In his own inimitab
pathy, Rev. Schul
travel down our pathway of trials and afflictions by giving wise insight and counsel.

Dr. Stephen R. Covey
Author of *The Seven Habits of Highly Effective People*
Cofounder/Cochairman, FranklinCovey Company

Turning Hurts into Halos is a fascinating book of true-life stories. It lifts the spirit, inspires the heart, and gives courage, enthusiasm, and hope to everyday life.

Ruth Stafford Peale (Mrs. Norman Vincent Peale)
Chairman of the Board
Guideposts® Magazine and Peale Center for Christian Living

TURNING HURTS INTO HALOS

ROBERT H. SCHULLER

DOUBLEDAY DIRECT LARGE PRINT EDITION

Publishers Since 1798

THOMAS NELSON PUBLISHERS®
Nashville

This Large Print Edition, prepared especially for Doubleday Direct, Inc., contains the complete unabridged text of the original Publisher's Edition.

Published in Nashville, Tennessee, by Thomas Nelson, Inc.

ISBN 0-7394-0550-0

Printed in the United States of America

This Large Print Book carries the Seal of Approval of N.A.V.H.

Dedicated
to
friends and family
who have
inspired me
to
celebrate
life
through
their
coming in and their going out,
In their
labor and in their leisure,
In their
laughter
and . . .
in their tears.

CONTENTS

ACKNOWLEDGMENTS

TO JEANNE SCHULLER DUNN, whose professionalism helped outline, organize all the subject matter, interview, and write the stories with heart and soul.

TO BARBARA EVANS, who took over 300 pages, handwritten on legal pads, and successfully put them on her word processor.

TO JANET HOOVER THOMA, Vice President at Thomas Nelson Publishers. They assigned the best to be my editor, and she became my friend.

TO MY WIFE, ARVELLA, who has edited my weekly messages for more than forty years. This was a good book when it reached her. By the time she finished, it was a great book.

Most importantly, to all of the silent, strong, suffering hearts whose stories are openly shared in this book to inspire, uplift, and encourage each of us to follow in their path of turning hurts into halos and scars into stars.

INTRODUCTION

THIS IS MY THIRTY-SECOND BOOK, and this book is for you if you are hurting—emotionally, physically, socially, spiritually, or financially. If you are suffering from painful realities, I want to try to walk with you to discover the positive possibilities in your adversities.

Yes, even if you are on a "happy, holy roll," this book is for you too. You are a human being, living under a certainty of unpredictable and unavoidable hurt. Call the reality mortality!

Wisdom dictates conditioning yourself for pain before it strikes you. For instance, every advocate of physical fitness disciplines himself with healthy exercise, sensible diet, and body care to prevent illness and atrophy. He exercises nature's latent powers to immunize the muscles and joints from the avoidable debilities of age.

Read this book and get into spiritual fitness. You'll be ready for life's inevitable challenges when they hit. Then when hurts inflict their unexpected and unwelcome pain, you'll be prepared to minimize their negative impact while you maximize your capacity to see and seize the positive possibilities in your pain.

And while you are living, laughing, and loving life, you will be protected from your greatest temptation: to forget that other people in this world desperately need the comfort and courage of happy persons like you. Someone somewhere needs help in his or her hurting. You may be the only one in a position to give a lift that can save this suffering person. Don't miss this silent cry in the night, or you'll miss earning life's most pleasant and proudest award. You'll treasure the profoundly satisfying tears that come suddenly when your eyes lock with the eyes of one who is moved by your compassion and you hear the words "Thank you!" from trembling lips.

Yes, this book is for you and for every living human being.

Believe me, this is a "good news" book! For I promise you that there is gain in every pain. All suffering can become a stepping-stone. All hurts can be turned into halos.

Through these pages, I will share with you some stories of people who have handled their hurts positively. Notice how they avoid anger, self-pity, or denial. "I'm the innocent victim" may be true, but it is not a smart or a wise reaction.

When I was the target of a gross injustice, I was asked by Larry King, "Do you see yourself as a victim?"

Instantly I answered, "No. What happened to

me is not fair. But I reject calling myself a victim. If I allowed that thinking to take over, I'd miss the chance to think creatively, redemptively, positively. I'd move downward to imagine *How can I get even?* instead of moving to the higher path of *How can I get better?*"

The ultimate solution to suffering is faith, and faith is a choice. I am a true believer in a God who loves me and wants to lift me. You may be an unbeliever. I challenge you to become a possibility thinker. That means you will leave the door of your mind and heart open to the possibility of this "God idea" being real and true, not mere fantasy!

I don't claim to know everything about God. I certainly don't have all the answers. But the little I know and follow makes all the difference in my world where I have to live.

Yes, you can draw triumph out of tragedy. This book also promises that you can create good news out of bad news! And when you discover the positive in the negative . . .

- You'll enjoy life again, not just endure it.
- You'll be spared from becoming a complainer and become an explainer—showing people in pain how to handle their suffering successfully.
- You'll become an inspiration! That's wearing a halo around your hurt.

Read this book collectively, not just selectively. You might be tempted to read the table of contents and grab hold of the chapter that relates to where you are: divorce, defeat, death, or dying. That's okay for a starter.

But I beg of you: read the chapters that don't seem to relate to where you are. It is amazing how hurts are so frequently interrelated. You may discover that while you thought you have worked through the hurts of a death or a divorce, you still have a hurt called loneliness or another hurt called emptiness, or another called failure, or another called depression.

Read the whole book. You may be surprised to find unexpected help and hope in the next chapter.

Where shall we begin?

I have found it immensely helpful to ask myself, "What's the worst that could happen to me? Can I handle that?!" If so, I can make my way triumphantly through anything. So we'll confront the worst hurt early in these pages.

You are embarking on a journey that will become the sublime adventure of your life. And you'll close the book with tears in your eyes and say out loud, "It's really true what Jesus said: 'If you have faith as a grain of mustard seed, you will say to this mountain, "Move," and it will move; and nothing will be impossible to you' " (Matthew 17:20 RSV). And you will say as Job said, "When He has tested me, I shall come forth as gold" (Job 23:10).

1

WELCOME TO THE HUMAN RACE

WELCOME TO THE HUMAN RACE! Are you hurting? Then you are truly human. Hurts are normal and natural—we can all expect them.

I was part of the fifteen-member presidential delegation that represented the United States at Mother Teresa's funeral in Calcutta. Led by Hillary Clinton, we visited Mother Teresa's orphanage.

"Dr. Schuller," one of the sisters said, "look what Mother Teresa had enlarged, framed, and hung in the front lobby here." The poem read:

ANYWAY

People are unreasonable, illogical, self-centered
. . . love them anyway.
If you do good, people will accuse you of selfish, ulterior motives
. . . do good anyway.

If you are successful, you win false friends and true enemies

. . . be successful anyway.

The good you do today may be forgotten tomorrow

. . . do good anyway.

Honesty and frankness will make you vulnerable

. . . be honest and frank anyway.

People love underdogs but follow only top dogs

. . . follow some underdog anyway.

What you spend years building may be destroyed overnight

. . . build anyway.

People really need help but may attack you if you try to help

. . . help people anyway.

If you give the world the best you have, you may get kicked in the teeth

. . . but give the world the best you have

. . . ANYWAY.

Insults, put-downs, and prejudicial attacks are epidemic in the human family. The result? Beautiful people experience undeserved hurt. Not even Mother Teresa went unassailed. I know how she must have felt.

I experienced a deep hurt when I was traveling to speak at Betty Shabazz's funeral.

An Unforgettable Incident

America was shocked when Betty Shabazz, the widow of Malcolm X, was the fatal burn victim from violent flames thrown over her helpless body by her sad and sick grandson. She lived a few horrific weeks in pain before dying.

I was honored when her family invited me to speak at her memorial service at the Riverside Church in New York.

Betty Shabazz was a heroic person to me. I watched how she handled the assassination of her husband, Malcolm X. She raised four daughters alone—each became a wonderful person! She went back to college and eventually earned her Ph.D. degree—and used it in such honorable social service.

Late in the day before my plane was due to leave L.A. for New York, Betty Shabazz's family called and asked me to take my clergy robe and wear it for the service.

"Take care you don't get it wrinkled, Bob," my wife, Arvella, reminded me as she slipped the gown into a plastic covering bag. "Hotels can press pants, but they will have to send the robe with its velvet decorations out to be pressed, and you won't have time for that! You get in late tonight and have to leave your hotel early tomorrow morning."

When I boarded the United Airlines plane, I hung my robe on the hanger behind my seat.

"You can't hang that there," the male flight attendant scolded me. "Airline regulations do not allow garment bags to be hung there." A female attendant reached out to grab it. "I'll put it in the closet up front," she said in the same unfriendly, condescending tone.

Concerned the crowded closet could crush and wrinkle the robe, I held on to the robe and restated my wish to hang it behind me, explaining the distance from the hanger to the floor was perfect!

"No garment bags are allowed there," the male attendant broke in again.

"But this is not a garment bag," I explained. "It's only a plastic bag covering my robe. In fact, I will take my robe out." And I did.

At this point, the attendant's anger was beginning to show in his voice and face. He turned, walked off the plane, and returned with an airline supervisor who smiled and said, "No problem, sir. You can leave your robe hanging there." I was relieved.

The attendant wasn't. He had been publicly overruled in front of all the other passengers.

All the way from Los Angeles to New York, my robe hung silently behind me. The male attendant could not escape seeing it. Hour after hour for the entire five-hour flight, it reminded him of his lost argument and public rebuke by superior management. His anger increased.

When he offered dessert—a plate of cheese with a few grapes—I requested, "May I just take the grapes please—without the cheese? I'm not allowed to eat cheese," I explained. "And it would be so helpful if I'm not tempted." I laughed. He didn't.

"This is the way it comes," he said, adding, "If you don't want it, I'll take it." Before I could respond, he grabbed it and was gone!

I went forward to the galley and asked a female attendant, "Could I possibly get some grapes please, without cheese?" She nodded and obliged.

Seeing me getting from another attendant what he had refused brought the male attendant to the galley fast. He confronted me and asked me angrily, "What are you doing here?!"

I reached out to calm him with a pastor's touch—open palms to the shoulders—when he jumped back and shouted, "Touch me again, and I'll have the pilot call the police to get you when we land!"

"I'm sorry," I said, stepping back and retreating to my seat. The young couple sitting in the front row only five feet from the scene saw and heard everything. They raised eyebrows, as I did, and we exchanged smiles. Without a word, I returned to my seat.

I thought nothing more about it. When the plane landed at JFK International Airport, no one was allowed off until a gentleman in a civilian suit entered the plane, followed by three New York City uniformed policemen. After speaking with the male attendant, he approached me and politely introduced himself as an FBI agent, then asked me to follow him. He led me off the plane, surrounded by the uniformed policemen. We entered a private room near the gate, where I was left in the company of the three officers.

The FBI agent informed me of a new federal law that any airline attendant who feels he or she has been assaulted verbally or touched in an unwelcomed manner by a passenger can order the pilot to call for law enforcement officers to meet the plane and remove the passenger. All fellow attendants were under orders to "agree" with any charges made by a fellow attendant against a passenger. I had walked into my first experience as the innocent victim of a humiliating, hurtful injustice.

I was detained for five hours while the FBI agent investigated the attendant's charge that I had "scuffled" with him, "shoving him back."

The FBI agent interviewed the female attendant and the other passengers—except for the young couple returning from their honeymoon, who chose not to get involved.

At midnight, the agent wrapped it up. "The attendant accuses you of physically shoving him. The female attendant, unfortunately for you, supports his claim, saying she saw your arms reaching out to him and saw him being pushed back by you."

"But I didn't push him. He jumped back!" I protested.

"Unfortunately, Dr. Schuller," the agent said, "since the attendant has a supporting witness and your word stands alone against these two, I cannot just dismiss it. I will have to turn this report in to the federal prosecutor to see if, in his judgment, there are grounds to charge you with a federal criminal offense. Where are you staying, if he chooses to contact you?"

I named the hotel.

"Then I'll let you go now," he said.

How often I've thought of the lines from Shakespeare I memorized in high school, "Who steals my purse steals trash; . . . But he that pilfers from me my good name robs me of that which not enriches him, and makes me poor indeed."

I caught a cab, went to my hotel, and, at one o'clock in the morning, went to bed.

Prayer time.

Then it happened! An experience of peace—deeper, purer than anything I ever experienced in my life. There was no anguish! No anger! No fear! No shame! No worry! I can only say I found myself absorbed by a holy peace. The message I felt was my acquittal in my judgment before the ultimate spiritual Supreme Court.

My Lord was there with a precious message for me: "You are innocent, Bob. Be at peace. Sleep well. Speak comforting words at the memorial service at Riverside Church this morning. All will be well."

I slept peacefully. I awoke to prepare myself for the service and, carrying my unwrinkled robe, went to the church.

The events of the night before paled in the presence of Coretta Scott King and Myrlie Evers-Williams (widow of Medgar Evers), whose husbands had been assassinated. Their spirit of love was an answer to prayer.

When I returned to the hotel, I was led to call a close friend, Terry Giles, who is a lawyer. He immediately advised me, "Bob, take the first flight home, immediately! The federal prosecutor may call you. If he does, you will have to go in and stand in line with prostitutes and rough people from the streets. You may be booked and fingerprinted in one of the toughest law enforcement departments in America."

"But couldn't I be charged with resisting arrest?" I asked.

"No way, Bob. At this point you have not been served."

One hour later I was on a nonstop flight home.

When I arrived there, it was late. Arvella hugged and kissed me. We slipped into bed, and it happened again—the sweet, still, pure peace that I can only describe as the presence of Jesus. God was with me, honoring me with the halo of His peace, purity, and holy presence.

From that moment on, the case was in the hands of my lawyer. He shared with me his discussions with the federal prosecutor. Terry Giles reported: "The federal prosecutor is in a delicate position. JFK Airport is in his district. If he simply dismisses the case when there are two witnesses against you, he could be accused of not supporting the airline people who so heavily populate his district. We have agreed that he can and will downgrade the charge from a felony crime to a misdemeanor. You could appear in court, plead innocent even to the misdemeanor, and request the privilege of offering an apology for anything you may have said or done to provoke the attendant. You will be asked to cover the financial costs the FAA encountered in their hours of investigation. You would only have to promise not to 'commit any crime for six months.' Then the case would be settled."

I agreed to do as Terry suggested.

"You will, as a matter of legal process, have to return to New York. The federal prosecutor will have to book you (privately, he assures me) and you'll have to be fingerprinted, photographed, and led to the judge. In a few minutes it will all be over."

That plan was carried out precisely. I returned to New York. With the respectful oversight of the FBI agents, I was driven by a private car to the courthouse and was led through the back door, where I pressed all ten fingers (twice!) on the ink pad, then stepped up for the mug shot.

And it happened again! Peace! The halo of His holy presence felt so, so good.

I smiled as the camera flashed. The FBI agent said, "This is the first time I've seen anyone smile for this picture."

He led me to the door. It opened to an empty room under the oversight of one marshal. We would have to cross this room to reach an elevator that would take us up to Judge Mann's desk.

"Where are your handcuffs?" the marshal asked.

"It's okay. No need for that," the FBI agent answered.

"No one crosses this room without handcuffs," the marshal ordered. An escorting policeman slipped handcuffs over my wrists and walked with me to the elevator.

The FBI agent could do nothing. Eight steps later I reached the elevator, and the FBI agent said to the officer, "Take those things off him!"

The attending officer obliged. So I had the experience of being briefly handcuffed. For less than one minute I tasted a humiliating hurt I had never tasted before.

The judge heard my attorney's word. Judge Mann forgot to ask how I was pleading. My attorney reminded her, and I pleaded "not guilty."

The courtroom was empty except for one reporter who got a scoop. The FAA charge was eleven hundred dollars. I wrote a check and left feeling like a free man.

When the news reached the attendant, he made the move we all expected. The story broke in the New York daily newspaper: "Airline attendant sues Dr. Schuller for 5 million dollars."

The young couple who had been with me on the flight saw the story. They couldn't believe it. When they heard I was on the Larry King show, they tried to call in to tell that they had seen and heard what really happened from their seats, only five feet from the galley. They failed to get through. The next day they called the Crystal Cathedral and were connected to my lawyer.

Kara and Dual Macintyre then issued a signed, written testimony that stated they witnessed the entire incident, and "Rev. Schuller did not hit or strike the flight attendant in any fashion. His actions appeared to be comforting and calming to an obviously overwrought flight attendant." They went on to state that the flight attendant was unharmed and that his service was the worst they had ever experienced. The Macintyres also signed an affidavit that they didn't know me or my ministry. (Thank You, Lord!)

With the criminal case behind us, the insurance company now took over to manage the civil case.

"Please don't pay them off," we pleaded.

Depositions were taken. Our defense deposed the airport doctor who had immediately examined the flight attendant after the alleged incident. He said in his report that he could find nothing to mark any injury or assault and concluded the attendant was healthy and could return to work. Instead, the attendant took the next twelve months off work as sick leave, claiming physical damages and seeking unnecessary medical attention.

My attorney assured me we would win a complete acquittal when the case came before the jury. Then my insurance company calculated their costs to continue to defend it all the way through trial. To save money, they made an offer to settle for much less. The flight attendant had no choice but to accept what little his attorneys and my insurance company agreed upon. The case was closed.

How can I thank the millions of people who believed in me after they heard the bad news when it first broke? How can I thank friends like Paul Harvey and Dr. Laura

Schlessinger for telling their huge radio audiences the day the story first broke that the charge of my assaulting an airline attendant was ludicrous? How can I thank Billy Graham, my friend for more than 50 years, who called to say he knew exactly how I was being assaulted by evil forces? How can I thank my Lord Jesus Christ for His presence and peace?

The answer came during my quiet prayer when I felt a strong message from Christ, my Lord: "Bob, you've been hurt. Turn your hurt into a halo. Now write the book that's been in your heart for many years."

WELCOME TO THE HUMAN RACE

When you were born, the meter was turned on. At unpredictable and unexpected times you will be called to pay the price of living as a mortal human being. No person escapes all hurts, whether deserved or undeserved. Everyone has hurts sometime, somewhere in life.

That's an assumption I've lived by. For nearly fifty years I have been a pastor to hurting people around the world. Few other professions face more hurting hearts than pastors. I've lived to call on people in hospitals, mortuaries, locker rooms, and courtrooms.

Believe me, I've been there. I have been with people who were where you are. And my mottoes have always been: "Find a hurt and heal it . . . Find a problem and solve it . . . Find a need and fill it." These mottoes have shaped and set the tone of my professional projects and preaching.

Again and again I've watched positive human souls come through horrific hurt to become inspiring heroes. That's when and where halos shine!

Divorce, murder, financial collapse, the loss of your name . . . yes, we will all face hurts somewhere, sometime, and to some degree in our lives. *Welcome to the human race*. The question is not, *Will* we face hurts? but *How* will we face our hurts? That is what this book is all about.

This is not a book of happy parties filled with loud laughter. Quite the contrary. Here we stand silently in the shadows, watching good people being overwhelmed by individual suffering that could engulf and consume them in undeserved and inescapable hurt. And we are astonished and inspired at the unquenchable, indestructible human spirit that gloriously emerges again and again out of terrible tragedies.

This book is not about a run in the stocking, a fresh stain on the tie, or a dent in the door of a new car. This is a serious book about heavy hurts. It is about adversity on the edge of disaster. This book is about the Cross.

A critic once told me, “I don’t read your books or listen to you, Dr. Schuller. You’re always playing the happy song. Try dealing with tragedy instead of triumph. Someday write a book on the Cross, and I’ll read it.”

So here it is. But to that critic I make a promise: every cross can be turned into a crown.

Somehow positive-thinking people survive through their shuddering suffering. Where does this transcending human spirit come from? We wonder as we watch them, broken and bleeding, rise on stumbling feet to stand up and struggle onward. Their awesome spirit is an inspiration to the rest of us, compelling us to downscale the disappointments and disasters in our lives, motivating us to make the best of our painful predicaments.

* * *

IT'S TIME FOR REALITY THINKING!

The shocking fact about Christianity is the blunt and bold honesty with which the followers of Jesus Christ recognize, without any rationalization, the reality of suffering in the human race.

For two thousand years Christianity has chosen the cross to be its symbol, held high and proudly as the flag of faith flying in the face of a suffering and tortured humanity.

The Judeo-Christian faith is blunt in calling us to the reality of injustice and oppression, evil and sin, sickness and suffering. Followers of the thirty-three-year-old Jew from Nazareth were so inspired by this young man's positive faith when He was nailed to a cross and died innocently in naked shame, that they launched a movement that would put the cross on the towers of church steeples around the world.

The cross has to be seen as the boldest, most beautiful "plus sign" in human history. Hope radiates with redemption from this stunning symbol. A shuddering minus has become a shining plus. That is the hope that radiates from the cross! At the foot of the cross, all hurt can be turned into halos.

What the world needed two thousand

years ago, it still needs today—a blunt faith that confronts the question of suffering, sin, and human agony. To the credit of Christianity, this intelligent and honest faith avoids fantasy and confronts the raw reality of human anguish and suffering. That is why Christianity has survived through famines, plagues, and holocausts.

Why Does God Allow Suffering?

Christians agree that there is no answer to *why?* Christians are realists. Reality thinking declares that life is made up of facts and mysteries. It is a fact that most suffering can be blamed on the sins of humanity.

The Bible paints blemished pictures of human beings; the Bible honestly tells the story as it is. A loving God created a gorgeous universe and crowned the beauty of this environment with honorable creatures called Adam and Eve.

Into this creative scene emerged the ultimate divine dilemma. We humans were designed with a spirit that can soar, a soul that can love, and a mind that can create, invent, and imagine positive possibilities. We were designed to be spiritual beings on a human journey.

Human beings were created as individuals, not as puppets to be manipulated by an almighty God. They were given decision-making power—the right to accept or reject divine impulses. These humans could not and would not be created to be computers, perfectly programmed and incapable of sinning. No, human beings would have the power and freedom of choice—they could choose to be good or bad.

God's purpose in creating humans was to create beings who could bring honor and glory to Him. Goodness isn't goodness unless it's a choice. Love isn't love unless it's a freely chosen option.

Here was the divine dilemma facing the Creator God: if He created such decision-making persons, then He, God, would take the ultimate risk in all creation. The risk was that these creatures called *persons* could choose to become selfish and sinful, capable of behavior marked by evil and injustice. This opened the door for hurt, rejection, and even death.

What is the answer to the ultimate question, Why does God permit and allow suffer-

> *Reality thinking is not "Why me?" Reality thinking is "Now what?"*

ing? The answer is a mystery. But we do know that God permits humans to experience hurts, rather than exercising His paternalistic power and extinguishing the personhood of human beings by removing their free will.

The *why?* remains wrapped in a mystery. The real question now begins with *what?* What is God doing about the sin? the suffering? the selfishness? the sickness? the death? What has He done? He has given all hurting human beings the freedom to choose to turn their crosses into crowns, their hurts into halos. With our free will intact, we can choose a reaction that turns torturous negative experiences into radiant positive ones that glorify and honor God!

So the final question is not a question you will ask God. The final question is one God will ask you: "What will you do—or what will *we* do together—with the hurt you face today?"

Now we turn reality thinking into possibility thinking.

Humans were designed by God to be His

angels on planet earth, where human suffering is a given. God is in the business of putting halos over human personalities. God is able to turn any hurt—even those caused by our own selfishness and sin—into a halo!

I do not know where you hurt today. I do not know why you hurt today. But I do know that each and every hurt you face today and in the future can become a halo.

Yet a halo is not secular self-achievement. No. A halo is a gift from God. To receive the gift is your choice, a choice to practice possibility thinking, even in the face of impossible hurt. An opportunity to never give up hope.

Never Give Up Hope!

This summer I listened intently to tragic and frightening news reports on our local southern California stations. An eleven-year-old girl had taken her dog out for a walk in her neighborhood. Mysteriously the dog returned home alone. The girl? Presumably kidnapped or worse.

Television reporters who covered the story interviewed again the father of Polly Klaas, the young girl who had been kidnapped two years earlier from her house in Petaluma, California, and was later found murdered. Marc Klaas, familiar with the pain and suffering this girl's family was enduring, offered these simple but profound words. "Never give up hope," he said. "Never give up hope." Mark Klaas has come through perhaps the greatest tragedy a person can face—the murder of a child—and now he is turning his horrific hurt into a halo.

On a more personal level, this year my extended family has known hurts. My ninety-eight-year-old mother-in-law passed away after a fulfilling and dynamic life. Her funeral was a celebration of life by her seven children, twenty-seven grandchildren, seventy-one great-grandchildren, and three great-great-grandchildren. But with so many at her service, a new hurt was exposed.

My nephew and niece, the son and daughter-in-law of my wife's brother, sat in the pews during this funeral, still grieving over the abrupt loss of their premature baby. Just weeks earlier, their tiny infant had given up her feeble attempt at life. Now as the soloist sang the words "How sweet to hold a newborn baby" from the hymn "Because

He Lives,"[1] my niece lost all control of her fresh grief.

How will she handle her hurt? How will the father of the missing girl handle his hurt? What hurts do you have that you must face today? I don't know what story you have to tell. I don't know how the final chapters of these stories and yours will be written. But the stories I will share with you throughout this book prove one thing: each and every hurt can become a halo.

How? In the upcoming chapters, I'll share with you the lessons I have learned after counseling hundreds of persons who have endured every imaginable hurt.

Let's search together to find a halo hiding in your hurt. It's there, really! You'll see! I firmly believe that each and every negative can become a positive. There is a halo in every hurt, and I intend to help you find yours.

But I need your assistance. Be open. Be pliable. Be honest. Don't expect me to change you. I cannot do that. Only you can change yourself. Only you can and will change how you respond to your circumstances.

However, I can and will show you:

- how to take your hurt off its life-support system
- how to keep your hurt from becoming a black hole (and the five dos and don'ts to make that possible)
- how to know if you are making it hard for people to help you
- how strength can come out of weakness if you follow four principles to turn your scars into stars

Along the way we will meet many people who have turned their hurts into halos.

Come join me on this journey. It won't be easy. It won't be fun. It may, in fact, be painful. It might bring up an old hurt that you thought was successfully buried. But it will be fruitful. It will bring the ultimate comfort.

Welcome to the human race. Let's get on with living. Let's discover how our hurts can become halos.

"Most people measure their happiness in terms of physical pleasure and possession. If happiness is to be so measured, I who cannot hear or see have every reason to sit in a corner with folded hands and weep. But as sinners sometimes stand up in a meeting to testify to the goodness of God, so one who is called afflicted may rise up in gladness to testify to His goodness.

The struggle of life is one of our greatest blessings. It makes us patient, sensitive, and Godlike. It teaches us that although the world is full of suffering, it is also full of the overcoming of it."[2]

—HELEN KELLER (1880–1968)
WORLD-FAMOUS AUTHOR
AND PUBLIC SPEAKER

2
How Heavy Is Your Hurt?

As I was preparing this book, I left on a trip to Asia, from Calcutta to Hong Kong, to visit cities where my weekly television program, the *Hour of Power*, is aired. My first night's stop was in Honolulu. As the sunrise was dazzling the eastern sky with dramatic color, I was walking alone on the peaceful, pure beach, reflecting on this book, when I met a woman with a perky golf cap perched on her head of well-grayed hair. She was taking her morning walk.

"Dr. Schuller," she greeted me, "what are you doing in Hawaii?"

I explained and then added, "And I'm working on a new book." Before she could inquire further, I asked, "Are you on a vacation?"

"Oh, no," she answered, "I was born here. My parents moved here from New York in 1938. I've lived here my whole life!" She was vivacious and enthusiastic. "Isn't this heaven!? How blissful, peaceful, tranquil."

With one arm she reached to the west, where the full moon was still glowing! And with the other arm she waved to the east, where the horizon beyond the perfectly-still ocean was ablaze with the orange colors of a sunrise being born.

"I sometimes feel guilty for living all my life in this precious place! What a great life I've had!" Then suddenly she turned her lovely, happy face, her warm and wonderful eyes locking with mine, and asked, "What's the title of your new book?"

"Turning Hurts into Halos," I answered. I quickly read her personality. The soft lines around her eyes were what I'd call "twinkle wrinkles." I was shocked when she impulsively responded, "I'll have to buy that!"

I couldn't comprehend her positive reaction. "But you've had such a great life. No hurts?"

"Oh, no," she corrected me. "I've had my hurts too."

"Forgive me if I'm impertinent or intrusive," I said, "but I'm into this book. I need to know where people are. What was—or is—your deepest hurt?"

"My divorce," she replied. "It was fifteen years ago. He was an alcoholic. He never would seek help. He lived and still lives in disastrous denial." Then she said something very profound. "The hurt that pained me so deeply was not what he did to me so much as having to see what he was doing to himself." She concluded with this insightful witness: "It hurts so badly to see someone you love hurting himself and refusing all efforts to be rescued from a path that leads to shame and ruin."

Before I left Hawaii, I connected with a friend known to millions as Famous Amos. This friend had a dream: to bake the best cookies and sell them! He founded Famous Amos Cookies and is known as the father of the gourmet cookie industry. Sadly, adverse financial conditions forced him to relinquish ownership of his company. Here's how he described the hallway of hurts he passed through:

"The financial collapse really hurt. I had nothing left, but I'd been there before and could handle that. Yet someone I didn't know acquired the brand name of my cookies, and I was told I could never use my name anymore, ever again.

"To lose your name is something else. So I decided to keep the positive attitude that had always worked for me. I started a new line of cookies and called them ‘Noname Cookies.’ ”

My friend turned his adversity into opportunity. He started another cookie venture, the Uncle Noname Cookie Company. Since then, he has written several inspirational books and has become one of America’s most popular motivational speakers.

Both the woman I met on the beach and my entrepreneur friend are beautiful personalities. In each case I saw a halo that crowned their spirit. They worked to get a proper perspective of their pain and hurt. That’s what I have tried to do since I was ordained as a minister in 1950. After nearly half a century in ministry, I’ve seen it all, I think, when it comes to human hurts.

A PROPER PERSPECTIVE

Yes, even the wars. I was in the main hospital in Tachikawa, Japan, which saw the wounded arrive from Vietnam. Before this I had walked the barren, battered hills of Korea where not a single tree was alive. All leaves had been eaten by the starving populace. All bark had been removed and boiled in water to make bark soup.

Now, finally, I am writing my insights, experiences, and impressions on how to handle the really hard hurts.

The first and most important counsel I can give is this: *get a proper perspective of your pain and hurt.* Here's where everyone—no exception—needs help.

To help you get a proper perspective of your hurt, ask yourself three questions:

1. How heavy is my hurt on the scale of human hurts?
2. How hardy is my hurt? What is its life span?
3. How healthy is my hurt? (It could be very healthy—even be spiritually nutritious. Or it can be sick, very sick, but curable.)

1. How Heavy Is Your Hurt?

No name in the Chicago media has been more celebrated during the twentieth century than a man everyone knew by the trade name Kup. I have been on hundreds of radio and television shows in my life, but one I shall never forget was Kup's TV show. I remember it because I felt I failed to help someone who was really hurting. Here's what happened.

Kup's wife was the producer. I greeted her in the green room with my usual honest enthusiasm. She was cool. It didn't take long for her to "spill her gut." She was angry. She was in horrendous emotional pain. She was—in her words—"an angry atheist." Her lovely daughter had been murdered senselessly, savagely, in Hollywood. With flashing eyes she said, "The worst hurt in the world, Dr. Schuller, is to lose a child. No child is supposed to die before her parents."

I have since recalled how many friends and acquaintances have lost children who were still in their young years! Art Linkletter—you'll read his story in this book. Gregory Peck. Tommy Lasorda. Entertainers have not been spared. We all cried when Bill Cosby's son was murdered.

Corporate chiefs with all their wealth have lost young children. J. B. Fuqua, a member of my board, lost his son in an airline accident, and Kim Woo Chong—founder of a great global conglomerate, Daewoo, and a member of my board—lost his college student son in a car accident. My friends the Ammermans lost both of their teenaged sons—one in a tractor accident and the other in a drowning on their Minnesota farm. Long ago I concluded that to lose a child is the heaviest of all human hurts. (I'll stand corrected in the next chapter!)

Now you have a hurt. A hurt that needs to heal. A hurt that needs to help you become a better person. Throughout the centuries, around the world, people have faced similar struggles. Possibly someone you know has faced the same hurt you now must endure. The shock always comes through in the thought, *I never thought this would happen to me.*

As we explored in Chapter 1, everyone everywhere faces a hurt that at first seems crippling. So the question is not *why me?* but *now what?* Let's start at the beginning of this task. Let's face the *now what?* with a good measurement of what you're dealing with. I know no better way than to put your hurt into perspective. For many of you, this very exercise will be the key that unlocks the door to surviving and succeeding despite your hurt. You may even come to feel, *Wow, I don't*

> *"My mother taught me very early to believe I could achieve any accomplishment I wanted to. The first was to walk without braces."*
>
> —WILMA RUDOLPH (1940–1994) OVERCAME CHILDHOOD POLIO TO WIN THREE OLYMPIC GOLD MEDALS IN TRACK

really have it that bad compared to what some people have faced.

For some, it will confirm what you already know—that your hurt is devastating. Your pain is a monster. It is among the heaviest of the heavy hurts in the human race. You will need all the support you can find to keep your feet on the proper path. So let's weigh hurts.

HOW HEAVY ARE LIFE'S HURTS?

For thirty years, I've been a television pastor to millions of people globally. Here is the "Hall of Human Hurts," which I've helped people get through.

- Death of a loved one
- Divorce or a broken long-term relationship
- Natural disasters: fires, storms, earthquakes, hurricanes, floods, etc.

- Tragic accidents: airplane crashes, ferry sinkings, train crashes, etc.
- Bombings, assassinations, terrorism
- Physical sickness, terminal or long-term suffering
- Suicides
- Loss of limb: amputations of legs, arms, hands, or removal of eyes, vocal cords
- Blindness, deafness, loss of speech
- Career disasters: ruined professions, unfair terminations
- Physical, emotional, or sexual abuse
- Financial collapse, bankruptcy
- Rejection or abandonment
- Injustice or exploitation
- Shame or public embarrassment
- Imprisonment by judge and jury

Now, you fill in the blank with a hurt of your own: ______________________. Or put yourself on the above list. Where is your hurt? Circle or clarify the hurt you have now.

Look again at the preceding list of hurts. Which do you think is the worst possible hurt? Rank the hurts from one to sixteen. Pencil in a number next to each hurt. Is suicide the worst? Give it a one. Is career disaster the easiest to handle? Give it a sixteen. Try to rank the hurts.

Why? Because then you can take a good look at your hurt and know where you stand in the heartache of humanity. You are not alone. You are surrounded with hurting people who have endured and survived hurts even heavier than yours!

I've had my share of hurts. Some of them have been ex-tremely heavy. Others seemed terribly hurtful at the time, but the wisdom of looking back today makes me realize how lightweight they really were! What seems like a horrible hurt today may become a lightweight hurt later in life.

Here's my list of hurts. Help me weigh them:

- When I was eighteen, my family lost our entire farm, including our house and livelihood, to a tornado. Everything was gone. But I went back to college and got a job as a janitor.
- A year later, at age nineteen, I lost everything I owned when my apartment building at college burned. To earn money for new clothes, I took another job and neglected my work in an English course.
- I got an F in that English class. "Stick to

speaking; forget trying to be a writer," my professor said.

- In 1978, my thirteen-year-old daughter, Carol, was in a horrific motorcycle accident that almost took her life (she required seventeen and a half pints of blood) but left her with an amputated leg.
- In 1958, I was put on trial by my denomination's court of church law. My young assistant leveled charges that I didn't preach the whole Bible, because I didn't preach "hellfire and brimstone." I was unanimously acquitted. He left the ministry, but it hurt!
- In 1979, my wife had breast cancer and a modified radical mastectomy. I'll never forget the telephone call from the doctor. "Bob," he said, "bad news. The lump was malignant."
- My son's first wife decided she no longer wanted to be married and divorced him. This hurt so badly, I preached a series of sermons on Job and put a marble statue of Job on our church grounds with this verse written in granite: "When He [God] has tried me, I shall come forth as gold" (Job 23:10 NASB).
- In 1991, I had an accident and nearly died of a brain hemorrhage. The neurosurgeon

told me if I had arrived twenty minutes later, I would have been DOA (dead on arrival). After two brain surgeries in eight days, I was okay.

- In 1997, I was falsely accused of assaulting an airline flight attendant.
- In 1997, I suffered a heart attack and underwent angioplasty.
- In 1998, my wife suffered a heart attack and had six bypasses. (This was close to a sixteen on the scale of human hurts! I thought I was losing her.)

I've had my share of hurts! I look at that list and think, *That poor guy! I hope he's okay now . . .*

I'm not only okay, I'm terrific. I have followed the teachings in this book and have had the luxury of years of learning from the greatest professors in the field of survival techniques: the great heroes in this book. As I mentioned earlier, it was right after the airline incident that I decided I needed to write this book. I was hurt. Deeply hurt. I felt assaulted. Unfairly accused. Lied about. *A victim of gross injustice!*

Wow! If I, the father of possibility thinking, was feeling like a victim, watch out! We're all in trouble. I needed to delve into the meat and potatoes of handling hurts so I could get over that seductive, self-absorbing, pity-party reaction. I was determined never to be victimized again—only victorious!

So I've weighed my hurts. And I've put them in proper perspective. Some will always be heavier than others, not because of the pain they caused at the time, but because of their life span. That leads us to the next part of this exercise.

2. How Hardy Is Your Hurt?

Each hurt has a different life span. When I look at my list, I think immediately of my daughter, Carol. Her hurt is always there. The loss of a leg for her has, in many ways, changed her life forever. It is a constant struggle for her to do simple chores and activities. But her attitude is fantastic. In fact, she doesn't appear to realize her limitations. She has made her hurt a friend. She never complains. She never says, "I wish I still had both my legs."

Divorce is a hurt with a long life span if children are involved. That's why Dr. Laura Schlessinger has made it such a strong part of her mission on the radio to challenge parents to remain committed in marriage despite struggles. Divorce is never final when there are children. There are always birthdays, graduations, weddings, grandchildren, Christmases, anniversaries . . .

The hurt from death carries a long life span. I remember interviewing Dr. Joyce Brothers after her husband, Milt, had passed away. She told me how she grieved for over a year after his death. It was annoying to her when well-wishing friends tried to hurry her through the grieving process, encouraging her to "get over him." She recalled how she felt so lonely that she thought life would never again be worth living. But, she said, day by day, little by little, life became better. She ran on automatic to make it through the day. Then one day, she found herself smiling again.

Yes. Hurts have different life spans. Receiving an F in college hurt at the time. But I really got over it fast! The tornado that wiped out our family farm was a tough one. My father was not a young man and had to rebuild everything. But the support of the local farming community was tremendous, and he opened his arms to the help they offered.

My wife's open heart surgery this past spring, as painful as it was, is already a thing of the past. The life span of the hurt of her heart attack is not as hardy as the osteoporosis she has battled for many years. My brain surgery in Amsterdam had a terrifically short life span because I don't remember any of it!

The point is, the pain you are feeling today, whatever your hurt, will pass. It will surely change. It may remain as a scar. But the life span of each hurt is different. Take a measurement and fast-forward to a year from now. How will your hurt affect you then? How will you have grown through this struggle?

Then consider taking your hurt off its life-support system.

TAKE YOUR HURT OFF ITS LIFE-SUPPORT SYSTEM

"Let go and let God" is a classic piece of therapy. Myriad psychological compulsions can operate to motivate persons in pain to keep their hurt alive. It is easy to blind ourselves and fail to see that the taproot of our hurt is long gone! We allow the hurt to live on in our memories. It's time to take the move and declare that old hurt dead and buried! (Good professional counseling can really be helpful here.)

The hurt is dead!

Take your hurt off life support! Quit carrying it around like a heavy suitcase full of all your disappointments, failures, guilts, and discouragements. You'll never know how heavy it is—until you stop carrying it!

You will feel the same relief I felt the day I stopped carrying my luggage. For many years when I was met at the plane by a friend or a welcoming emissary, the person picking me up would offer to carry my luggage. I always refused politely, thanking them for the offer. One day I shocked myself and said, "Yes. Thank you! That would be very nice!"

I handed a heavy carry-on bag to my new friend. For the first time in my life, I walked off an airplane with nothing to carry! I can't tell you what freedom I felt. Only moments later a stranger recognized me in the airport. He asked, "Dr. Schuller, may I have your autograph?"

My hands were free to oblige, so I said, "Surely! I'd be delighted." I didn't realize how restrained I had been by my own baggage. I didn't realize how heavy my luggage was until I stopped carrying it.

DON'T BE A BURDEN BEARER

My first trip to Jerusalem was nearly a quarter of a century ago. I was so shocked when I saw human beings carrying huge posts, probably ten feet long, on their backs. They walked bent-backed under their enormous loads. I learned that these people were called burden bearers. I remembered reading about them in the Bible, for the Bible is full of burden bearing.

Twenty years ago I visited Korea. Again, I saw human beings using their bodies to carry huge collections of packages on their backs. One farmer in Korea was walking home at the end of a day, ahead of his oxen. The farmer was carrying the plow. A big, heavy plow. Behind him trod the oxen.

I said to my guide, "Why doesn't that farmer let the oxen carry that plow for him?"

"Oh," my Korean host said, "the oxen have worked so faithfully all day that the farmer will carry the plow home for them." Burdens, loads. Everybody has them.

One of my favorite Bible verses is 1 Peter

5:7 (RSV): "Cast all your anxieties on him, for he cares about you."

How heavy is the luggage you are carrying today? How long have you been carrying it? And why don't you accept the offer of relief that God gives you?

Sufferings, sorrows, setbacks—these are all burdens that we need to let go of. The name Richard Neutra, the architect of the Tower of Hope on my church campus, is well-known among architects throughout the world. I asked him one day, "Richard, have you had any disappointments in life?"

"Yes, I have."

I said, "What were they?"

He paused for a long time. Finally, he said, "First of all, I have never received the recognition that I feel I deserve from my own profession. I have received a gold medal from the President of the United States. I have received gold medals from Japan, Austria, Germany, and Switzerland, but the American Institute of Architects has never recognized my work."

"Why not?"

"Well," he replied, "I think it's because I'm from California, and some of the people in the East have a prejudice against the art that comes out of California."

A few years later he died, and I conducted his funeral. Seven years after that, the American Institute of Architects gave him the gold medal. But he had carried that snub, that slight, all his life. He never could let go of that luggage.

What sufferings, setbacks, slaps, insults, or injustices are you holding on to? What negative comment did a high school or elementary teacher make about you that has held you back? What label did you accept that now keeps you from even trying to break out of the mold that someone who really didn't know you put you in?

My daughter confessed to me that she really insulted a friend of hers when she was a young girl. The friend was the assistant pastor's daughter at our church. Together the two girls enjoyed the youth choir. But suddenly the friend dropped out. She never continued in the youth choir program, which provided a lot of fun and travel experiences later in high school. Years later the friend commented to my daughter, "Yes. I dropped out of choir because one day you turned to me and said, 'You can't carry a tune.' "

What unhealthy comments are you holding on to? Was it something your spouse said? Or was it your overly critical mother or demanding father? Perhaps someone told you, "You are *never* good enough" or "you *always* overreact."

Get rid of it! Get over it! Give it up—to God!

"Cast all your anxieties on Him!"

What secret are you holding on to that you are so afraid someone will discover? Who will discover it—your husband? your parents? your children? your boss? What sins have you committed that have yet to be exposed and forgiven, or for which you have yet to forgive yourself?

Give it up—to Jesus Christ!

"Cast all your anxieties on Him."

Only one leader of any religious movement had scars in the palms of both hands. He is the only person who claimed to be sent by God with the authority to forgive people for their sins. Give your baggage to Him.

When we were building the campus of the Crystal Cathedral, we included a beautiful tower, the one Richard Neutra designed. We crowned the tower with a mighty ninety-foot cross. The reason was simple: We wanted to tell the world, "God loves you! He offers Jesus Christ as the answer to your hurts, your concerns, your scars, and the burden of your baggage!"

Two beautiful pieces of art hang in my office. Besides their artistic quality, I treasure them for the message they bring me.

One is a painting of Christ praying in the Garden of Gethsemane just a few hours before He was tried and crucified. His face is full of agony. His heart looks broken. It is a painting full of despair. His words, recorded in the Bible, describe His anguish: "Father, if it is Your will, take this cup away from Me; nevertheless not My will, but Yours, be done" (Luke 22:42 NLJV).

The other painting is a picture of the famous golden eagle, Freedom. An Iowa farmer found Freedom flopping in a snowy field December 30, 1980. The mighty eagle had been shot in the wing and left to die. The farmer took the hurting bird to the Raptor Clinic at the University of Minnesota. The clinic nursed that eagle back to health. Thirteen months later, Freedom was flown to Washington, D.C., on the occasion of the American hostages being released from

LET GO AND LET GOD

As children bring their toys
with tears for us to mend,
I brought my broken dreams to God,
because He was my Friend.
But then, instead of leaving Him in
peace to work alone,
I hung around and tried to help
with ways that were my own.
At last I snatched them back and
cried,
"How can You be so slow?"
"My child," He said, "what could I do?
You never did let go."

Iran. He was later released back to the wild. Slowly and awkwardly, he spread his six-foot wingspan and soared upward to the sky. Soon he was soaring silently overhead. Freedom!

Yes! You, too, can have freedom from the anguish, the vengeance, the hostility, the insults, the sufferings, and the hurts.

"Cast all your anxieties on Him, for He cares about you!"

3. How Healthy Is Your Hurt?

Hurts can become the taproots of seriously sick emotions if these hurts are rooted in our reckless behavior and carry with them well-deserved shame. Contrition, repentance, and apologies must be applied honestly, humbly, and swiftly.

Or hurts can be healthy. Grief can be sweet sorrow if the tears are an outpouring of love for someone who is gone. If the hurt rises from healthy and happy memories, it can be a spiritually and emotionally healthy experience.

How will you handle your hurt? Let me share a true story that may inspire you to become an "undergoer" who becomes an "overcomer."

GLORIA KING PUT HER HURT IN A POSITIVE PERSPECTIVE!

Gloria King is a mother who knows what it means to endure a hurt with a long life span! This courageous woman recently sent me a lengthy letter detailing her amazing story. I tried to cut it down, edit it, and retell it myself, but it doesn't grasp the full complexity of her own words. She gives me too much credit, but she grasped what I've been trying to do all my life in ministry. She turned her hurt into a halo!

So here's her letter, one of the most powerful letters I have ever received:

In every mother who lost a child, and every mother who nurtured a child of special needs, there lies in her mind a book that tells a story the world should hear. I suppose I could write that book, but I realize it would be repetitious of so many thousands of books on heartache and triumph. Mine would differ only in one way. I would attribute any success I might have enjoyed in mothering to, of course, my faith in God and love of Jesus, but also the sustaining power in a dear stranger who guided me from his pulpit, thousands of miles away. He was a beloved friend, father figure at times, partner in pain, and always present in our laughter. He was constant . . . always there for me and my son . . .

This tribute is to two of the most loved, important people in my life—my son, Jeff, and you, Dr. Schuller.

First, I can't say you introduced me to Christianity. You did, however, save me from losing the faith.

After marriage I went on a church search with my husband, trying to find a good compromise, and sadly found nothing really worked. It became a very tough bone of contention. My husband attended the baptisms of my first and second children, but never with an open heart or mind. He is dead now, and I realize he was in so many ways a good man, and I forgive him. It was the birth of my third child that put me to a test I never dreamed I would have to take.

Our son was born with spina bifida and given about three days to live. My husband was numb. He could only run from this thing that was hurting him so. Somehow, I learned to care for this fragile little life and busied myself in keeping him alive night and day. I was so preoccupied, it never occurred to me to take time to pray. If I had a moment of silence or peace, I tried to sleep. I guess I never really noticed that my husband was gone! So were my home and security. I had three small children, one severely handicapped, and a very judgmental, old mother.

As the children grew, I took them to Sunday school, taught them to say grace and nighttime prayers, but mostly out of duty. I was pressed on a daily basis, answering my son's needs and medical emergencies, and making ends meet. I am sure God heard my few fervent pleas, but failed to hear many thanks. For what? Many times physicians gave me another grave prognosis, and I took it upon myself to prove them wrong. And as I look back, I see the "footsteps."

One Sunday morning about twenty-some years ago, I bathed Jeff and sat him in his wheelchair to have breakfast in front of my babysitter, the TV. I tuned in and this great voice came through and resounded these words, "This is the day the Lord has made! We shall rejoice and be glad in it!" The sun was shining and I thought . . . why not? It's quite beautiful today, and Jeff seems to be feeling good. Even the laundry is caught up, and we have a roast for dinner! I settled on the couch and listened . . .

For many Sundays I made it a point to find this TV preacher because he could make at least one day of the week seem okay. Jeff was drawn to his twinkle and kindness and seemed to understand the message. Not long after, Jeff would say on Saturday night, "Be sure to wake me up for the Hour of Power." Mom and Jeff were hooked on this feel-good feeling! Soon every day was a day to rejoice and be glad in. We often joked that our joy was due to our Sunday morning Wheaties and breakfast with a champion! Jeff began to grow in wisdom and spirit.

We watched you build the Crystal Cathedral and the Walk of Faith. We watched the children grow and marveled as we heard young Robert preach his first sermon. We suffered and had firsthand understanding when your daughter lost her leg. (Jeff also had both legs and thighs amputated.) It was then Jeff learned how to allow himself to weep out loud and chant "Alleluia . . . Alleluia" when he was in very devastating pain.

We prayed for your wife in her illness and kept vigil for you when you suffered your head injury. You became a very close part of our family.

Each morning I would walk in Jeff's door and sing Mr. Rogers's tune, "It's a beautiful day in our neighborhood." Sometimes it would be a dreadful day, and often Jeff was in a hospital room, with few things that looked beautiful, but somehow God just put that little tune in my heart so we could at least TRY! Jeff always laughed, pointed his frail little finger at me, and said, "Yes, God loves you and so do I!" He used all your little phrases through his life when they were appropriate. "Inch by inch anything is a cinch" . . . "Keep on keeping on" . . . etc., etc. He kept a pad by his Bible on the bed tray and wrote the Bible passage for each Sunday so he could read it and ponder it later. He also wrote down the (as he called it) Schuller punch line of the week.

We often wished we could afford to have our name engraved on a windowpane of the Cathedral, or send an enormous check that put our name on an appointment to the church. And the eagle . . . how we loved that eagle! . . . We even daydreamed of buying a new pew seat and wondered how they wore out so fast and then realized how many years we had been attending Sunday service! We never had money, but somehow we were always able to scrape together our wee tithe hither and yon and send our mite. And the blessings grew!

One day Jeff received a treasure! A small medal from you. "When faced with a mountain . . ." and you know the rest. He wore that medal for probably seventeen years. About four years ago his brother faced the reality of alcoholism and was forced to join AA. I was devastated, until Jeff removed the medal and presented it to his now very struggling, sober brother. He carries it in his pocket at all times. But, that was only the beginning.

We still sent occasional small gifts whenever possible and always received beautiful letters of thanks. One Christmas season Jeff needed his first leg amputation. For no reason whatsoever and from out of nowhere, he received a beautiful golden bell to hang on the tree the morning of his surgery! We both forgot to be anxious, and they wheeled him down the hall clutching his precious bell! And the stories never cease . . .

One year you came to Toledo to do a book signing of the Be Happy Attitudes*. Jeff begged to attend (not an easy feat). At that time he was into clay sculpture and his sculpture was quite primitive, but he made a shepherd, and it was fired and painted. Jeff wanted with all his heart to present this little gift to you. Under protest, but with great understanding, I bundled him up, loaded his chair, and scraped together the money for the book. The line was unbelievable!*

Jeff clutched his shepherd, and I could almost feel his little heart beat as I teetered from foot to foot, looking for a bathroom and praying you would accept this humble little gift and shake Jeff's hand.

From nowhere, once again, a man in a suit came over and said, "Follow me." We were swept past the throng of people, and the suited stranger just handed Jeff a book and pushed him up to your table! I froze . . . I could not believe what I was seeing! Jeff put out his hand and gave you the shepherd. I felt a tinge of embarrassment.

Then I saw you rise and kneel beside the chair, and you and Jeff prayed. I never knew the prayer or asked. I allowed it to belong only to Jeff. We left with the book, inscribed to Jeff, "Keep on keeping on. I love you, Robert Schuller." It was from then on that Jeff felt this wonderful personal relationship with you, who had taught him so much about Jesus and how to walk the walk of faith, even without legs.

Then came the Sparrows Club. It seemed that was meant for us! We could never have an eagle, but we could surely be sparrows. My sense of humor makes me want to relate that as I wrote the first check, I chuckled and thought, "If he only knew it's more like the old crow and the ugly duckling sending this off!" It made Jeff so happy to be part of the ministry. My greatest treasures now are my bookends, the music box, the crystal apple filled with seeds of wisdom, and, most recently, the sparrow jewel box. But, it's the eagle . . . the coveted eagle you must know about . . .

Jeff pursued art very early on. For the most part it gave him a reason to rise and often the stamina to work into the night. He was encouraged by a local, now very well-known, artist in Santa Fe to have a one-man show. I was aghast at the very thought! He is too sick!! He's not that well-trained! All negative, but kept inside. I encouraged him each day, never dreaming what would transpire.

Soon Schuller Goal Sayings were plastered all over his wall. I would peek at his journal and notice that he was very confident that his show would come into being! He struggled for three years with dozens of medical setbacks, including a three-month stay in ICU. His therapy afterward was learning how to hold a brush again. He persevered! He just kept on keeping on! I can't recall the effort now, but I know the chore of putting on this one-man show was horrendous! But I admired him so much I wanted it to be grand!

As we addressed formal invitations to the opening day, Jeff said, "Don't forget Dr. Schuller."

Quite taken aback, I laughed and said, "Jeff, I think you are looking at your first impossibility."

He replied, "Never mind, I'll do it," and mailed off his invitation with a letter and the hope that you would recall the shepherd. He also informed you that the show was named Wind Beneath My Wings because of the beautiful words of Isaiah and his belief in them. He certainly had waited and worked diligently toward this goal, with the inspiration he heard each Sunday.

I chuckled and sent a mother's blessing on that letter as I dropped it in the mailbox. I recall thinking, We must have the faith of a child! A few weeks later, a box arrived for Jeff. The letter attached to the outside expressed regrets that Dr. Schuller would not be able to attend the gala because it was on a Sunday, but enclosed was a gift and he hoped apologies would be accepted . . . the eagle! Jeff's coveted eagle! The words he lived by, inscribed on the base!

True to Jeff's luck, all that could go wrong that day went wrong. He became very ill and septic early in the week and fought so hard to get well by Sunday! The gallery was hung, the invitations were out, food was prepared, and even a tuxedo was ordered for this grand occasion. There was no way to call it off.

I paced, panicked, and prayed and prayed! Jeff in his pain and feverish despair mumbled on Friday, "I got that eagle, didn't I? By Sunday I will fly!" . . . Saturday night I left the hospital in total despair and noticed a swift change in weather. I intended to just go to the show on Sunday and apologize.

A blizzard hit Toledo! By six A.M. on Sunday, roads were treacherous! I stood at my window and cried. The phone rang at seven A.M. My heart stopped with fear. It was Jeff's doctor. He said Jeff was sitting up, and his fever had gone down a bit. He told me to have my oldest son deliver the tux to the hospital, and the nurses would get Jeff dressed. The doctor had already arranged for the ambulance and would leave emergency lines in his veins. He said he would accompany Jeff with some nurses and I should get myself ready . . . the show would go on!

As I look back, I can't fathom how this all came together! Jeff looked radiant as he welcomed and shook hands with at least 150 stout-hearted folks who weathered a severe storm and treacherous roads to attend. And again, from nowhere, came the media. Channels 11 and 13 covered the show, and Channel 11 came back later to do a story. His show of twenty-four pieces was sold.

As the ambulance driver lifted a very exhausted body from the wheelchair to the stretcher for the trip back to the hospital, that frail little finger pointed at me again . . .

As I kissed him, he managed to laugh and then said, "Oh, ye of little faith!" We both laughed so hard! He was tired and very weak when they loaded him into the ambulance, but he raised that frail little finger and once again pointed to me. "Go home and rest, Mom. God loves you and so do I."

I have sent some newspaper clippings to attest to his success and document the truth of my stories and also to brag a bit. I hope you will indulge me.

Yes, I could write a book. Twenty-seven surgeries, the pain of diapers at age ten, the struggle to master braces, and then defeat due to scoliosis. Eighteen years of dialysis. Amputations, infections, heart failure, even waking up during surgery and not being able to motion for help. The miracle of an abscessed kidney just rising to the surface for the apprehensive surgeon. The miracle of surviving the flesh-eating microbe that killed Jim Henson that same week. I watched this little bug at work on Jeff's belly. I watched Jeff fight and come back to do his show. How did he finally die after thirty-five years, when the doctors said he would probably live three days?

I think he was tired and quite satisfied

with his accomplishments! I think he had whatever prayer Dr. Schuller whispered with him as he breathed his last. I usually tell folks he just laughed himself to death . . . At his funeral two years ago, I somehow gathered the courage to set the mood and deliver a message of hope, not despair—joy, not sorrow—a day of celebration of Jeff's new birthday as I returned him, well cared for and loved.

I thanked God for the blessing of knowing Jeff and choosing me to serve him, and then I surrendered him. To a shocked gathering I returned to my chair and gave Jeff a thumbs-up and contemplated the many "footsteps."

So many others had so, so much to say. Jeff just attracted people. He was truly loved. Few ever noticed his affliction. He had a way of making people feel good. He stole all of your lines and practiced all of your philosophies. It was decided to end the service with the song "Wind Beneath My Wings" . . . There were no dry eyes, and I did weep! But I recall hearing the words and saying, "This one's for you, Schuller . . . this one's for you!"

As I wander now in my lonely little apart-

ment, I often touch my treasures. I have a fridge magnet that says, "This is the day the Lord has made"; three beautiful Christmas angels, my sparrows, and, of course, the coveted eagle. Through the many years you have given me so many things that I lost track of many.

But the journals, Jeff's journals, are my greatest gift. They are filled with inspiration and hope. They are a collection of "Be Happy Attitudes" and excerpts from your books that he read and applied to everyday living. Many times he wrote . . . "I feel like crap! I am so sick and tired . . . I think I cannot wait another day for my kick in the pants from Dr. Schuller. I will try my best to hang on, hold fast, and tune in. I will be OK . . . nothing is impossible!"

I am now filled with time and spend many hours in deep prayer. I pray daily for forgiveness for my past impatience at times, and forgetfulness of His tender mercies and, of course, my transgressions. But . . . prayers have changed. I almost never have an urgent plea. It is always a prayer of thanksgiving for all He has given me and entrusted me with. I thank Him for carrying me and recall every footstep. And I never fail to thank Him for sending you into my life and helping me teach Jeff how wonderful life can be! It seems I worked and worried a lot . . . God carried the burden . . . and YOU took this beautiful creation and gave him meaning and joy! I just had to thank you! But . . . I am but one sparrow (or old crow) who has a story to tell about you! Because you are still my dearest friend, and I feel the relationship that Jeff felt as you humbled yourself by his chair, I will keep on keeping on!

I received a letter this week from Jeff's former doctor, Dr. Ronald Shapiro. It seems he was able to locate and procure two of Jeff's paintings. He intends to have them hung in the waiting room of a new dialysis center in Toledo. A tribute to Jeff's spirit and an "inspiration to all who must be there." I am so proud! Thank you so much, Dr. Shapiro! Thank you, dear Lord! And thank you, Dr. Schuller, who helped make this life so wonderful!

Gloria King never put her hurt on life support. No way! Instead, she saw her hurt not as a hurt but as a challenge of life, a commitment of caring, a sacrifice of service. Her hurt became her halo.

3

Life's Heaviest Hurt—Abandonment

I LEARNED YEARS AGO to face each crisis, hurt, or tragedy with these basic questions: "What's the worst that could possibly happen? Can I handle that?" If I can face the worst that could possibly happen to me, then I can face anything!

So what is the heaviest of all human hurts? My answer? Abandonment. If you learn how to handle that hurt, then you can be spiritually empowered to turn any hurt into a halo.

Let's start with a man who experienced the worst of all human hurts and lived to tell us about it.

"I can tell you about human hurts. I believe I have experienced all of them." The speaker at the dinner I was attending was Elie Weisel, a survivor of what history recalls as one of the most horrific episodes on planet earth.

The Holocaust. "The Ultimate Solution," Hitler called it. This evil anti-Semite conceived the demonic scheme of terminating the Jewish race. Concentration camps were built. Jewish people—old, middle-age, young persons, even children—were loaded like animals on freight trains and hauled to their prisons. A number, tattooed on their arms, replaced their names. They were placed in poison gas showers to be systematically executed. Scientists, doctors, religious leaders, Grandparents, artists, musicians. No one knows how many were exterminated. It is estimated that well over six million people were gassed, burned, shot, or starved to death. Loaded railroad cars came from all over Europe: Germany, France, Holland, Poland, Czechoslovakia, Hungary, and Austria.

There were survivors. More than one person would be saved and set free and then escape to America or Israel, their new nation. More than one of those victims would become my friends—most notably the psychiatrist Viktor Frankl.

Elie Weisel was a Holocaust survivor. Pain, suffering, and death were all around him in those unspeakable days of indescribable horror. "I went through all of it," he continued, "but the worst of all came when I felt that no one knew I was still alive. I was sure that everyone I had ever known had given up on me. I felt abandoned—and that was the worst of all human hurts."

Yes, abandonment is life's heaviest hurt. I've also heard that from prisoners of war who were locked in "tiger cages" in Vietnam. "The worst torture," they would recall later, "was to be cut off from all fellow prisoners and be told repeatedly by our captors, 'No one believes you are alive anymore. They have forgotten about you!' " Day after day, month after month, the abandonment horror was the torture that allowed the brainwashing to happen. But again and again the imprisoned soldiers who believed in prayer never felt completely abandoned. They believed that there was a God—somewhere—and that He could hear them!

Children even experience this greatest of all hurts.

Those Who Extend a Hand

Unfortunately, abandoned children are found all around the world. One of my dearest friends was Bob Pierce. He became a Christian as a young teenager and dedicated his life to being a missionary. He studied, was credentialed, and boarded a boat to China, alone, to seek his spiritual place in God's good work. Walking on a street, he noticed another American holding the hand of a little Chinese child. As they searched each other's eyes, she spoke first, "I can see you're an American. What business are you in?"

"I'm here to be a missionary," he answered naively.

"A missionary?!" the rugged lady inquired. "I'm a missionary too, with the Reformed Church. What mission are you with?"

"I'm here praying for guidance," he answered. "I'm looking for my mission. I'm just connected with God."

"Then take this child. He's an orphan. Abandoned. Doesn't belong to anybody. Here! He's yours! Take care of him!"

She simply put the boy's little hand in Bob's and left them behind! From that encounter was born what has become the world's largest and most respected mission to orphans, refugees, and famine-inflicted nations in the twentieth century—World Vision. God reached out to an abandoned nameless orphan, using the heart and hand of Bob Pierce. That hurting and homeless child trusted the outstretched hand, and that became the beginning of something awesome! When that child responded with faith and trust, I think the angels in heaven saw a halo glow over Bob Pierce's heart!

Another friend of mine, Bill Wilson, was himself abandoned as a child. Bill remembers:

"I was just a little kid when my mom said, 'Let's go for a walk,' " Bill remembers. "She came to a spot in the street and stopped and said, 'Sit here. Don't move. I'll be back . . .' I waited all day, all night. I slept there on the street. For three days and three nights I waited, but she never came back.

"Then a nice man stopped and asked me what I was doing there. I told him and he said, 'Well, come along with me. I'm a Sunday school teacher. Come on. You'll like it. Are you hungry?'

"He fed me. He took me to Sunday school, where I was told about God and Jesus. I became a Christian. And I decided I'd spend my life helping abandoned kids."

That's the true story of my friend Bill Wilson, who has organized the largest Sunday school in the world, including the abandoned kids. His school buses pick up children by the thousands, many of them unwanted, and bring them to his mission in the slums of New York—up to twenty thousand kids gather there every week. Bill still drives a bus himself every week he's in town. He drives slowly, his head and eyes shifting sharply and swiftly down the sidewalks and alleys, looking for stray kids.

"You know, Dr. Schuller, who I'm looking for?" Bill asks. Then he answers, "I'm looking for me!"

Bill Wilson has turned his hurt into a halo. So can you!

God is alive, alert, and roaming the streets and alleys of the world. He is living in human beings of all colors, cultures, creeds, and credentials and is reaching out to adopt the spiritual orphans into his family of faith.

Abandonment. That is one hurt I have never experienced. But my Best Friend did—and He, with His horrific hurt, and the halo that radiated from His having lived through abandonment, has been the single most definitive experience of my life.

My Best Friend's name is Jesus.

He was born a Jew. He was brought up in a good Jewish family. He lived the faith. Through the centuries He has become in history the morally and spiritually Ideal Person. His life was unstained by selfishness or sin. He would experience the hurt of rejection, grief, humiliation, injustice, broken bones, and a body stabbed by spear and nails—left bleeding to die a slow death, hanging on a shameful cross between two crucified criminals. At the young age of thirty-three he would die in disgrace and dishonor. His body would hang naked in shame, and His soul would be stripped of all holy pride. He would experience real hell when His innocent heart cried out, "My God, My God, why have You forsaken Me?"

And the God He loved, lived with, and served so obediently, never answered this painful question.

Why? is the one question all innocent persons in pain cry out to the blackness that is deathly silent. *Why?* is the one question God is not obligated to answer. The truth is, when in our pain and hurt we call out "Why?" to God, we don't want an answer. We want out of the dark place. If God answered, He'd be drawn into an argument.

His answer would only provoke more questions from us, "But why *me!?* I don't deserve it."

Why? is the normal, understandable, proper, legitimate question, but that doesn't mean it is the right question. God wanted to teach this basic, fundamental lesson to all humanity once and for all—that the questions that start with *why* may never be answered. This is why He allowed the most beautiful Person of all time to ask "Why?" and teach us that the almighty God does not need to answer.

So long as the *why* is unanswered, we are compelled to trust God in times of agonizing mystery. If and when acceptable answers could be offered by the eternal God to His human creatures in suffering, we would know the meaning of pain and would become more dependent on always demanding answers; we would become even more addicted to reason—and that road leads to the atrophy of faith.

We must come to the mental maturity that confronts agonizing mysteries with the positive attitude: "I don't understand—but I believe in God anyway."

Faith grows through trusting God when

we can't see or find answers. Winston Churchill, prime minister of England during World War II, once said: "I can handle any hurt and can accept the worst except a mystery. A mystery I cannot accept."

Wrong, Mr. Churchill. For all of life is a mystery!

Mystery Is the Ultimate Reality

What, after all, is a mystery?

- A mystery is recognizing realities that defy explanation.
- A mystery is asking questions that cannot be answered.
- A mystery is confronting challenges that confound empirical analysis.
- A mystery is the humble confession that we don't have all the answers, and some of our answers may be wrong.

A mystery is a gift of God's grace. It's His strategy to shape us into maximum personhood by molding us into positive-thinking individuals. That means we move into mental maturity when we are shaped into a character who "keeps on keeping on," "moves ahead," "Waits patiently," and "trusts anyway." That's the process of growing into mature adulthood! So every mystery is a God-given opportunity to become a bigger, better, and more spiritually mature person.

To trust while you are in the midst of the swirling currents of ambiguity is a high-water mark of mental, spiritual, emotional, psychological, and religious health. Mystery, then, is the arena where an empowering faith can emerge and evolve. Faith grows by asking intelligent and sincere questions. As the famous poet Alfred, Lord Tennyson, said, "There lives more faith in honest doubt, believe me, than in half the creeds."

Mystery is also the arena where positive science and positive theologies can meet. One of the greatest American physicists in history, Dr. Edward Teller, was a key scientist in ushering in the atomic age. He was brilliant as he shared with us, the members of the American Academy of Achievement, and three hundred of the brightest high school seniors whom we had invited to our annual conference. Sitting bent-backed in his older years, his walking stick balanced between his knees, Dr. Teller wrapped up his challenge to the best and the brightest,

"Become scientists, and all your life remember these words: '*I don't know*.' "

Beware of any person in any profession who impertinently assumes he knows it all. Accepting mystery as the ultimate reality is to touch the edge of divine love. Now we are in the process of evolving into humble humans! Now we are on the path to becoming healthy and helpful, religious and scientific creatures. Now the door is open to seek, see, and size up the power of faith—the intellectual stamp of wisdom.

Now watch the mystery become a miracle! Move ahead with quiet trust, and you will turn the hurt into a halo. So without an answer to His question, "My God, My God, why have You abandoned Me?" Jesus grasped faith at the highest level. He referred to His father as "heavenly Father." Quietly He spoke once more: "Father, into Your hands I commend My spirit." And the hurt turned into a halo. In this positive reaction to awesome pain and suffering, Jesus Christ became my holy hero!

Yes, heroes are people who hold on to hope through their horrific hurts, even though they don't get answers to the toughest questions like *why?* or *where?*

THE TOUGH QUESTIONS

"Where is God?" and "Has He abandoned me?" are two other questions commonly asked by hurting people.

Where is God when we can't feel His presence? He is in people. Trust Him! He sends people who affirm their love to you. Yes, people you never knew before. Have you experienced the loss of a loved one, a father, a mother, a child, a spouse? Did you receive a medical report that you have cancer? Have you had a breast amputated, or have you picked up a terminal disease?

As a pastor, I have heard countless people say, "What shocked me was who called me." "I got a letter" (or "I got a telephone call," or "Somebody spoke to me"). "Somebody at work, even though we never talked, heard what I was going through and met me at the water cooler" (or sent a note, card, flowers, or cookies).

What were these people doing? They were being an expression of the presence of a comforting God. Where is God in the worst of hurts? He is finding persons whose hearts and minds and hands He, the eternal

> *"God will not permit any troubleS to come upon us, unless He has a specific plan by which great blessing can come out of the difficulty."*
> —PETER MARSHALL
> PASTOR, CHAPLAIN OF U.S. SENATE, AND AUTHOR

caring God, can use to touch your painful heart.

Where is God? Wherever He is, He has not forgotten His promise: "Fear not, for I have redeemed you; I have called you by your name. You are Mine. When you pass through the waters, I will be with you. And through the rivers, they shall not overflow you" (Isa. 43:1–2).

My daughter, Carol, called upon this promise after she was in a motorcycle accident at age thirteen.

The accident happened in Iowa, and her left leg had to be amputated. From Iowa she was flown by a private hospital jet to California and brought to Children's Hospital in Orange, California.

Day after day, night after night, twenty-four hours a day, either her mother or father was with her in her hospital room. We slept in a chair with our legs extended over a stool. She was never left alone.

Then more surgery was required. A horrible, painful infection raged through her shattered thigh. Ghost pains flashed. The suffering of our child, an innocent victim, was heartbreaking to watch. She lived—but! I recalled the words from a Greek tragedy where the surviving lover looks at the dead body of his spouse and wails, "The death thy death hath dealt to me [abandonment!] is greater than the death thy death hath dealt to thee." Often the hurt of the caregiver is more painful than the hurt of the care receiver.

Inevitably the time came when Carol had to be left alone at night, so her parents could go home and sleep in their own bed.

That night came. My wife said, "Carol, I think you'll be all right without me tonight. If you need the nurse, ring the bell. I'll be back tomorrow morning."

"Oh, I'll be all right, Mom! Go home and sleep."

For the first time in several weeks, Carol, still in isolation, found herself alone in the darkened room. Then the morbid mood of a fear of abandonment stealthily moved across her suffering body and soul.

In Carol's own words: "The hum of medical equipment beeped its vigil watch. A low-density light from the hospital hall testified that the activity there never slumbers. That light now crept into my room, reaching its gaunt and ghostlike fingers across the one leg tucked beneath the coarse, generic, very impersonal bed covering.

"The artificial quiet that did exist somewhere between the beeps and the hums carried its own buzz. You know that sound, when quiet is so quiet that it *screams!* That lonely is so lonely, it *stampedes!*

"I was clinging to my favorite, floppy, sworn-to-be-real pooch (though its heart lay buried beneath manmade stuffing). Its brown velvet nose was wet with tears, which came from the trauma that had bullied me in the past. I attempted to turn on my side in a desperate search for pretended confidence. But instead I discovered a mere desperate longing. And then they came again, those wet, salty, uninvited droplets that revealed the plight of my soul. First one, then another found its rest on the familiar landing of my pooch's worn velvet nose. His heart, surrounded by fluff, was pressed against my heart, which lay broken beneath the blood and pain. 'Come, Jesus! Come Jesus!' was my simple prayer.

"Then, as suddenly as the darkness and silence came creeping, something very beautiful hushed the terror. Jesus came. And I felt as if He lay right behind me and wrapped His arms about my trembling torso. He spent the night with me. Now, years later, in my nighttime I continue to experience the comforting presence of Jesus."

Followers of Jesus Christ have believed for two thousand years that He was crucified—but resurrected on Easter—and lives today and can and does connect with people who cry out to Him. I embrace that faith and promise you that in that powerful faith, you will never, never, never be abandoned.

So don't yield to the negative, unfounded assumption that there is no God—or that He has abandoned you because He doesn't answer the three toughest questions you can ask:

- *Why* is this happening to me?
- *Where* is God? Has He abandoned me?
- *When* will my suffering end?

We often ask: "When will help come?" "When Will this pain cease?" "When will my faltering faith be restored?" When? was the question asked again and again by the Old Testament prophets who wondered if God had forsaken them.

God makes no promise to answer the when question, for the same reason God never answers the why question—He knows we could not understand and would not accept His answer. We would only argue instead of trusting patiently and quietly.

God has never—anywhere in the Bible—promised to answer these three questions: *why? where?* and *when?* Questions that start with these words are seldom answered.

But God hears and answers questions beginning with *how?* or *what?* These questions sincerely seek wisdom and guidance.

How, O Lord, can I handle this? *How* can I go on positively? *How*, O Lord, can I believe that You do know me and care about me? *How* can I turn my hurts into a halo? And, *How* will You help me to become a better person through my pain?

What? is another question God often answers. Questions that start with *what*—like questions that start with *how*—are humble questions that, instead of provoking argument, sincerely suggest a willingness to invite and follow divine guidance. God promises to give us guidance, often with a holy hint from heaven.

The Guidance of a Hint from Heaven

A really special friend in my life was Viktor Frankl, who at the time of his death was the leading psychiatrist in the world. Viktor was known for his Logotherapy, which focused on *logos*, the spirit of the human soul. He believed that the human being is the only creature on earth, unlike all other animals, to have a spirit. Because humans have this spiritual dimension, Viktor believed that psychiatry cannot be based just on chemicals or drugs.

As a Jew, Viktor believed in God. He was practicing in Vienna when anti-Semitism was spreading fast. Every Jew had to wear a yellow star around his neck, including Dr. Viktor Frankl. His father and mother said, "Viktor, you've got to get out of Vienna. There is an opening at Columbia University in the United States. Apply for it; maybe you can get it. It could save your life."

Viktor sent off his application. Some weeks later he went to the post office to pick up his mail, and there was a letter from Columbia. He opened it . . . *You have been accepted.* He was ecstatic. He could escape. The Nazis would let him leave the country if he was going to teach at the prestigious Columbia University.

On the long walk back to his office, Viktor thought, *If it had not been for my father and mother, I wouldn't have this letter.* Then he began to think, *What's going to happen to my father? What's going to happen to my mother? Should I leave them alone? Can I abandon them?*

As he struggled, he prayed. *Should he go to America or shouldn't he?*

He arrived at his office, and one of the other doctors said to him, "Oh, Viktor, I found something for you. I walked by the synagogue that they bombed last week, and I found one chunk of marble, unbroken and uncracked. It is the capital letter of one of the Ten Commandments. I laid it on your desk."

Viktor walked into his office, and there on his desk, carved in marble, was the capital letter of the commandment "Honor your father and your mother, that your days may be long upon the land which the LORD your God is giving you" (Exodus 20:12). Viktor said, *"That was my hint from heaven. I could not abandon my father and mother."* He tore up the invitation from Columbia, stayed, and was captured by the gestapo. He honored his father and mother.

Not long after the gestapo captured him, they made him take off all his clothes. "Strip naked," they commanded, to see if he was circumcised. That was all the proof they'd need to "prove" he was a Jew. Then one of the gestapo noticed he was still wearing his wedding band and ordered him to take it off and hand it over. In that moment, as he slipped the ring off his finger, God came into his mind with this thought: *There is one thing no one can ever take from me, and that is my freedom to choose how I will react to what happens to me*.

That single, spiritual concept was the revolutionary power principle that caused Viktor Frankl to react positively to the worst suffering possible. *I can find some meaning in the darkest night,* he thought. In the years of horror that followed in the concentration camp, he developed the most powerful philosophy of psychiatry, which he called Logotherapy.

Viktor Frankl lived through the Holocaust. He lifted the profession of psychiatry to a spiritual level. And he died at the age of ninety-two.

The long and painful process of turning his hurt into a halo started with what he called "his hint from heaven."

Another friend of mine, Mother Teresa, listened to a hint from heaven to rescue the abandoned.

When Mother Teresa died in India, the press called me and asked how we became acquainted. I met her first through the books of Malcolm Muggeridge, one of England's super-sophisticated intellectuals and a top-rated television commentator. At one time he was an unbeliever, a cynic, and an atheist. Then he heard about a Catholic nun who had opened a home for the dying in Calcutta. Curious, he checked her out and heard this story:

Walking down a street, Mother Teresa saw a dying person lying in the gutter. Everyone walked around him. Rats ran over him. He was left to die alone. Abandoned.

No one should die alone. This holy hint

from heaven consumed the mind of the nun who had only one coin to her name. She stooped down and dragged him into an empty building and cleaned his dirty, dying body. She stroked his fevered face and watched him die. He passed away, experiencing peace in the presence of God that emanated from this solitary sister of charity.

When Malcolm Muggeridge visited Mother Teresa's home for the dying, he was overwhelmed by a spiritual presence in that place. He was "consumed by the love of Jesus Christ, who was living in these sisters of charity." He was clearly, quietly, uncompromisingly convicted. "I met God then and there," he told me.

Years later I, too, would visit Mother Teresa's home for the dying in Calcutta. No one in human history did more to focus attention on abandoned humans than this simple, small-framed person who was literally under the control of the Holy Spirit coming from the heart of her living Savior, Jesus Christ.

She not only provided a home where the terminally ill could die in the presence of God's love, but she also had an orphanage for abandoned children. An open window faced the street (in the same way that open windows in drive-in hamburger places in America allow food to be passed through to customers outside). Only here, the open window was for people to pass through their unwanted babies or children! There were over four hundred babies, toddlers, and infants in that orphanage when I visited it.

Years later I met Mother Teresa in Tijuana, Mexico, where she had set up a home for the poorest of the poor. In our visit the subject of the Crystal Cathedral came up. Mother Teresa knew the story of how I started a church with only one member—my wife. With just five hundred dollars I could not find an empty hall to hold services. In desperation I went to a drive-in theater, where for over five years I would stand on the rooftop of the snack bar, preaching to people in their cars. It would be a defining period in my life, for I fell in love with the sun, the sky, the birds, and, yes, the rain falling on my open umbrella as I prayed and preached.

Twenty years later, to accommodate our ten thousand members, I needed a roof over their heads. I needed to raise money to build a church. "But I'm homesick for the sky," I said to architect Philip Johnson. "Can't we let the sky shine down on us? Can't we make it out of glass?"

Then and there the concept was born. The Crystal Cathedral would be built of ten thousand windows. From the inside we'd be able to see the sun and the trees through the windows. From the outside, the windows would be mirrors reflecting the real world around us.

From this idea came an inspiring prayer: "Lord, make my life a window for Your light to shine through and a mirror to reflect Your love to all I meet."

I expected Mother Teresa might criticize our spending money on a large glass church. Would she echo the challenge I had heard from people in America—"Why didn't you give that money to feed the poor?" Instead, she affirmed my mission: "I'm saving people from physical starvation. You are saving them from emotional starvation." Then she added, "Dr. Schuller, I want a copy of your Crystal Cathedral prayer. Write it out for me, please." Then she handed me a small piece of paper. I wrote the prayer and handed it to her.

After she folded it up and placed it in her tunic, I said, "Now you owe me one,

Mother!" She laughed and wrote out a blessing I keep framed with our picture together: "Be all and only for Jesus. Let Him use you without consulting you first."

Trust God, and somehow, through someone, sometime, or some way, God will reconnect with your stumbling, struggling soul! Suddenly a door opens, and you will not feel abandoned anymore. That is real salvation!

- A brave new idea will emerge.
- Opportunities will rise out of your adversities.
- Strangers will enter your life to become new and best friends.
- A renewing faith will stir and grow within you.
- Miracles will be conceived and born out of grueling mysteries.

God has succeeded! He has achieved His glorious goal—to make you into a true person, a trusting human, a powerful spiritual being.

Hurts? They still happen. But you will look into the dazzling darkness of God and know that something good will come from this!

Your cross will turn into your crown.

You will understand, "Life's not fair, but God is good!"

Now liberated from the imprisoning mental attitude that demands provable reasons for every element of faith, you become a truly whole and spiritually healthy human. The chains of cynicism are broken. Your mind is open to reach exciting possibilities even before they are probabilities. Your thinking becomes moldable, pliable, and receptive to the greatest idea ever to enter the human consciousness: There is a loving, caring God after all!

You have embraced a new lifestyle! It's called living in faith. Yes, the mystery becomes a miracle. You will never be abandoned again, for you are mentally, spiritually, and emotionally connected with your Creator.

Now you can handle any hurt!

Abandoned?! Look for God living in people who are letting God's love flow from their hearts into your spirit. Trust them. And become an adopted member of a worldwide family of God!

"You must not think that I am unhappy. What is happiness and unhappiness? It depends so little on the circumstances; it depends really only on that which happens inside a person."

—DIETRICH BONHOEFFER
LUTHERAN PASTOR, THEOLOGIAN,
AND OPPONENT OF NAZISM

4

How Are You Handling Your Hurt?

Sooner or later, wisely or foolishly, with or without caring friends, you will be left alone with your hurt. Make friends with it. Let it turn you into a kind, compassionate, caring person, and it will become the best friend instead of the worst enemy in your life.

If not, your hurt can become a horn.

Hurts are normal and can be handled—unless they cause you to take your eyes off your good goals. Hurts are a part of living. But instinctively they can be turned into horns that embroil the human spirit in anger. As a pastor, I've seen it often as anger against God. The horns wore the symbols of:

- Ill-tempered aggression
- Defiance (unwillingness to accept personal responsibility for managing their own reactive behavior)
- Defensive blindness to the whole picture. (The hurt is only one part of a larger picture.)

- All enthusiasm is gone. The drive to achieve has disappeared.

IS YOUR HURT A HORN?

Once a hurt becomes a horn, it becomes a destructive and negative influence in your life. Whether rational or irrational, it seeks to bring hurt to others, regardless of whether they deserve it. It lashes out at those who would seek to help you. A horn is an ugly outward expression that guarantees the hurt will not heal. It will not become a halo.

Karen raised her children with a 1960s type of love—lots of feel-good philosophies and "it's-okay-if-it-doesn't-hurt-anyone-else" values. Her daughter, Kelly, was especially beautiful, and the hard-working mother held her in high esteem. Kelly attended the town's most prestigious prep school with dreams of a college degree. Karen worked extra jobs, cleaning homes and making homemade jams to supplement her husband's construction income to pay for Kelly's expensive education. Karen's hopes were high for Kelly to lead a better life than her own. Nothing could prepare

Karen for the serious pain that her daughter would both create and endure.

Through a series of disastrous choices and misplaced values, Kelly tragically became involved with a drug dealer. What began as mere trysts with drugs became a full-blown addiction. During their shared highs, the man she lived with would often beat her to a pulp. Kelly would come home bruised and battered, promising never to return to him again. But after a few days, she always did, enticed by a new car or extra cash, which proved to be the appeasing ingredient in a dangerous relationship.

Karen was beside herself. She had not raised her daughter this way. She had nurtured her in a loving home. Yet all of the pleading, family intervention, and even counseling proved fruitless. Regardless of Karen's actions, Kelly always went back to her drug dealer lover, only to return a week or two later, bruised and crying.

For her mother it was an explosive situation. Anger that welled up from the hurt inside her created a living monster. She couldn't work. She couldn't sleep. She could only think of one thing: getting revenge on her daughter's abusive boyfriend.

Karen put her thoughts to action. She stalked the boyfriend. She bullied him. "Hit me!" she taunted him. "Hit me and I'll hit you back!" On one occasion, she found his parked car and spray painted it with the words *abuser* and *drug dealer*. Each time, she gave in to her anger and hurt and let it overcome her good sense.

This tragic outcome has not been fulfilled in either a good or bad ending. It simply endures. The daughter, who held such promise, simply muddles along, unable to hold down a job. Her mother continues to seek revenge, hoping to aggravate the situation by entrapping the boyfriend into doing something punishable by prison. Whenever this mother speaks of her daughter, her eyes flash with rage. "I'm never going to give up," she says. "I'm going to get him yet!"

Clearly, Karen's hurt has become a horn. Despite counseling, she has refused to give up the anger. She owns it and, in turn, it owns her. Although she cannot change her daughter's situation, she could change her own. She could let her hurt start to heal, but it has no chance of doing so as long as she seeks to strike out. Her hurt has consumed her heart with anger.

Ask yourself the following questions to determine if your hurt has become a horn:

- Have you surrendered leadership of your life to your hurt?
- Is your hurt leading you to anger? Jealousy? Depression? Discouragement?
- Is your hurt lying in the shadows of your collective memory, giving birth to an illegitimate assortment of fears, resentments, disappointments, anxieties, and morbid moods?

Then your hurt has become a horn, just like one prominent man I know.

His Hurt Became His Horn

I cannot tell his name. His story is too painful to publicly disclose. I can share his hurt only by couching the details to protect his anonymity. His hurt is as fresh today as it was the day it happened, decades ago.

It's the story of a prominent man, a respected and revered man, known for his laughing eyes and tall spirit. Yet under the twinkle and good looks is a hidden sorrow.

Years ago, when he was in Europe for

work, he received a phone call from his son. Distraught over seemingly unsolvable problems in his life, the son attempted to get his father's attention. "I have a gun, Dad," the son said. "I'm going to kill myself."

The father was shocked and panicked. "No, son!" he screamed as he heard a shot ring out through the phone line. A moment passed and, as the father wept, he heard his son's words through the earphone. "It's okay, Dad. I didn't shoot myself."

A few hours passed, and the son called again. For a second time he tormented his father, "I'm going to do it this time, Dad," he claimed. "I'm going to shoot myself." A second time a gunshot rang out. Again, the son spoke once more. He was still alive.

For a third time, the son telephoned his father. "Dad," he said, "I hate my life. I want you to come home. I need you."

The father pleaded with his son. "You know I can't come right now. I have to work."

"Then that's it!" the boy declared. A third time the father heard a shot ring out.

This time the son never spoke again. And the father knew the hideous truth. The police arrived at the scene and found the body.

Across the room they found two slugs from the earlier shots, lodged safely and deliberately in the wall. The third was a point-blank shot to the head.

This scarred father has never been able to fully overcome the tragic loss of his son. It has become a black hole where he has forever lost a part of himself.

Not long ago, I asked him if the hurt moved farther into the past as the years went by.

"Never," he said. "There is not a day that goes by that I don't feel like I've been kicked in the stomach by a horse."

Is Your Hurt a Black Hole?

If you are not careful, your hurt can become a black hole that sucks all enthusiasm out of life and suffocates new dreams God wants to give you.

THE HURT OF VIETNAM

Let me call him John. He went through the horrific hell of war in Vietnam. He came home alive but emotionally and physically scarred. The orders and commands of superior officers who sent him into battle left him an embittered veteran. He would forever resent, resist, and react negatively to "superior" advice and supervision.

This negativity has affected every area of his life. Eventually, his marriage failed and ended in a sad divorce. His hurt became his horn as he moved across the country from one job to another.

Finally, John was offered a wonderful job in a caring, compassionate institution. But eventually, even there, his deep-seated unhappiness surfaced. When supervisors counseled him, he took the counsel as criticism. He never lasted long in any department. State and federal laws would not allow the company to discharge him, so he was moved from one department to another. He soon earned a reputation as a high-maintenance person. Finally he was left working as a janitor in an isolated corner. He'd been left to live alone with his hurt and its litter of negative emotions.

> *Wounds don't excuse you of assuming responsibility.*

He had allowed his hurt to become his horn and lead him into a black hole.

John is a tragic illustration of one who was innocently kicked in the teeth and suffered a horrific hurt that was not of his doing. He could not control the visions of death and destruction that were hurled upon him at a young and fragile age. He could not excuse himself from the horrific hurt of war. No, he was violated by graphic combat. But the greatest injury was not what the war did to John. The greatest injury was what John did to himself. He let his hurt control him. He nursed it. He held on to it. He wrapped himself up in his hurt and let it become the excuse for all his failures. How did the hurt cause more hurt? Simple. *His hurt had become a deep, black hole!*

I am often asked about some of the tougher issues facing society today, like assisted suicide. I ask, Is this issue attempting to change a hurt to a halo? If not, forget it!

Assisted suicide could be the ultimate black hole. Dr. Jack Kevorkian is betting on the frailty of the human spirit. The option to quit. The inability to persevere. At best, Kevorkian inspires others not to hold on, not to hold out, and not to express courage.

The problem is that you and I do not know what medical breakthroughs are right around the corner. What pain-control

> *Assisted suicide won't inspire to aspire. It will only inspire to expire!*

medications are being reviewed by the FDA today that might be on the market tomorrow? What family members or friends are able to help today who were not available yesterday? What caregivers will there be who weren't resourced before?

Don't let your hurt become a black hole!

- Is your hurt restraining or restricting the birth of fresh enthusiasm and new goals?
- Is your hurt lurking furtively in that deep, black hole in your subconscious where it swallows the seeds of new dreams before they are even conceived in your imagination?

Most of our heavy hurts never die; they just lie around, waiting to be aroused by a new relationship, a new risk, a new frustration, or a new opportunity. Face it—if you cannot kill a hurt, try to fill it with a new spirit. You can give your hurt a new heart.

You Can Give Your Hurt a New Heart!

There is almost always guilt mixed in the heart of every hurt. "If only I had . . ." or "If only I hadn't . . ." Hurts are hard, if not impossible, to handle by persons who fix the responsibility and blame for their sad, sick, or suffering experiences on themselves, on others, and even on God!

Why do intelligent persons avoid the personal responsibility to confront their hurts with honesty and humility? Try *guilt* as an answer to these questions. Not always, but often it's the right answer.

Suppose that our universe is a spiritual as well as a material universe.

Suppose there is a God who is the Creative Genius behind this universe.

Suppose that this God wants to send redemptive ideas, constructive dreams, and creative concepts into human minds but finds these persons rejecting His signs and signals because of guilt.

Then what would God do? Provide a universal, eternal Savior who could contact and connect confidently with any human being, and in that interfacing, the Savior could get the garbage of guilt out of the heart.

You can give your hurt a new heart when you give your hurting heart to Jesus Christ!

Now that's a saving software every human computer needs!

Suppose that Savior pardons, forgives, saves, and redeems that hurting heart, and fills the living hurt with a new compassion. Christ fills the hurt with a deep caring for other suffering souls.

A new conception generates a new direction! "In love's service, only broken hearts will do."

Reach out. "I've been there . . . and I care" is the new spirit given by Jesus Christ. Then you are born again. That's what happened to Sebastian Yeo, a young man imprisoned in Singapore.

He Turned His Hurt into a Halo

I am a great believer in prayer. My life has been a life of prayer. As a pastor whose televised church services are seen around the world, I often receive requests for prayer for people I have never met. I know prayers are answered, so I try to respond and pray with and for people when I get the chance.

In 1997 I received a request for a letter and prayer from a man in Singapore whose brother was in prison. The young letter writer, Joe Yeo, informed me that his brother, Sebastian, was on death row for involvement with drugs. I have traveled to Singapore many times, so I was not shocked that a death penalty was the sentence for drug trafficking there.

I wrote the requested letter to Mr. Yeo in prison and then forgot all about it. Just recently, I received a follow-up letter from his brother, Joe. In it, he informed me that Sebastian had indeed been executed. Among the belongings still in his brother's possession was my letter. The truly amazing part of this story is not that the man would keep my letter, but rather that he would keep it until his death and become a blessing to millions of people! How? Read on!

But first, start at the beginning. Read the following letter I sent to Sebastian Yeo in 1997, the one he kept until the day he was executed.

Dear Sebastian Yeo,

How very saddened I was to learn of

your current situation from your brother, Joe.

When tragedies hit, people ask, "Why?" God never gives us that answer directly, but He does give us the faith to believe that in everything He works for good and that we can turn a tragedy into a triumph. May the following words of our Lord bring you comfort and strength:

> *"I am the resurrection and the life. He who believes in Me, though he may die, he shall live." (John 11:25)*

I can only imagine your loneliness and fear as others appear to be holding your future. But comfort yourself in the knowledge that only God holds the future. He truly loves you. He could send an angel to deliver you from prison. Or He may be calling you to face this all the way through.

Please know that you are prayed for. Let this letter encourage you in your faith. Don't let go of your faith! Wrap yourself around the knowledge that He cares for you!

I ask the Lord to reach deep within you where only His finger can reach and touch your heart and leave behind a fingerprint of peace that nothing can rub off!

God loves you and so do I!
Robert H. Schuller

Now here is the letter I received from Sebastian's brother, Joe:

Dear Dr. Schuller:

On November 14, 1997, you have written a letter to my brother Sebastian Yeo at my request to encourage him (a copy of your letter is enclosed). Now, I am representing my entire family to thank you for this letter.

As you may recall, Sebastian was arrested on January 8, 1997, and convicted on July 4, 1997, of drug trafficking. His appeal on September 24, 1997, was also dismissed. His final chance for clemency from the President of Singapore was also denied on August 22, 1998. The mandatory death sentence was carried out on August 28, 1998, at dawn.

When Sebastian's belongings were returned to us on August 28, 1998, we discovered your letter. The entire family is most grateful for your letter to Sebastian.

I believe your letter had definitely encouraged Sebastian in November last year. It also encouraged us tremendously. We have shared your letter to [with] members of our Bible Study group and they, too, were greatly encouraged.

We have also enclosed a copy of Sebastian's last letter to our family and a photo of Sebastian taken two days before the execution. I hope to share with you the last days and moments of Sebastian's life so that it may be an encouragement to you and your ministry. I would like you to know that your letter of encouragement written to someone you do not know, of another culture and of another country, has a wonderful ending too.

Monday, August 24, 1998, was the designated day for us to visit Sebastian. He had already sensed in his spirit that he would be called home soon. When he confirmed with us that the President's clemency was denied, he told us what to expect. He even knew that he would be executed at dawn on Friday. He began giving instructions to me, telling me what to expect, what I ought to do. He also wanted to donate his organs after his death and sought my mother's agreement. As you can see, Sebastian was ready to be with the Lord and was just settling his earthly duties.

From Tuesday to Thursday, the family was allowed to visit once in the morning and once in the afternoon for a period of two hours each, with three visitors at one time. It seemed so short and insufficient, but its impact was great. For the next three days, Sebastian was encouraging the family, speaking with full confidence of knowing God personally. He was reminding us to trust in God totally, comforting us that all things would come to pass. My mother was greatly comforted by Sebastian's faith and trust in God! There were tears but there was tremendous peace, too. For my family members who have not accepted Christ, Sebastian prayed and hoped for their acceptance; for those who have believed, he hastened us to grow in the Lord.

At the last half hour, the prison warden allowed six of us to see Sebastian together. My eldest brother, Isaac; myself; my two younger brothers, Kent and Jeremy; my mother, and Sebastian's fi-

ancée, Grace, were with him. With God's strength and grace, we were able to sing "Amazing Grace," "Majesty," "In Christ," "We Are One Family," and a Chinese worship song with Sebastian. There were tears, but we also derived great comfort from the songs we sang. That was how we parted from Sebastian; it was the last time we saw him alive.

We were told later by Rev. Khoo, the prison chaplain, that even on the way to the gallows, Sebastian was able to joke with him and sing "Amazing Grace" over and over again. Rev. Khoo has shepherded Sebastian, baptized him, and walked with him all the way to the gallows. My brother's last concerns were for my mother and his fiancée, but "Amazing Grace" was on his lips as he breathed his last. Praise God!!

When we look at Sebastian's photo, taken two days prior to his execution, we see the confidence, peace, and readiness to be with the Lord. Reading his letter further reiterated his trust in our Lord. He wrote as if the Lord was guiding him with such confidence and conviction.

Our entire family agreed that Sebastian's letter to us should be used as a testimony to be shared with others. We hoped that Sebastian's letter could be a means to achieve his heart's desire to reach out to lost souls. With the help of our church, Sebastian's letter was typed out and copies were made; it was also translated to Chinese, and we placed them everywhere through the wake services for all family, friends, and relatives to read.

For this same purpose, we hope that Sebastian's letter will be of use to your ministry. It may have seemed a small act on your part when you wrote Sebastian, but it has contributed to a wonderful ending for God.

Yours sincerely, Joe Yeo
for the entire Yeo family

When Jesus Christ entered the mind, heart, and soul of Sebastian Yeo, He truly changed Sebastian. It was a real conversion! Did He take away the punishment for the crimes Sebastian had committed? No, but He gave Sebastian the grace and the peace to accept the finality of his sentence with the true dignity that comes only from the Lord!

Here is Sebastian's final letter, which was printed in mass quantities to be distributed on the day of his execution. It has been read on the *Hour of Power*, and is reprinted in this book, and I am sure it will be read by many around the world!

Hello. By the time you read this, I will have been with Jesus for a few hours already. I want to thank all of you for your kindness, love, and generosity. I am proud to be a member of this family. As all of you know, I could have escaped during the day of my arrest. If time could turn back, I would still choose to stay.

I love you all very much. I can't thank God enough for what He has done for me.

My calmness came so naturally to me during the last few days, it shocked me that I have no words to express. I assure all of you, that not once was there fear nor regrets. The Lord kept me humorous, joyous, and peaceful. It is an indescribable feeling. I can't ask for more at this point of time; the Lord has answered most of my prayers.

I am sure the Lord will lead all of you through these difficulties when your trust in Him is total. Because of my trust and belief in the Lord, I am able to look forward to being reunited with all of you in the Lord's king-

dom. It might be many years for you before all of us will be together in heaven; for me it is like the twinkling of an eye.

My hope, of course, is for Kent, Ricky, and Rocky to receive the Lord, and for the rest to testify to others and continue to grow in the Lord's gentleness, kindness, and love, which is forever.

Please assure Mom of my well-being and ask her to remember what I shared with her. I will ask the Lord to let me be your guardian angel if it is possible.

Thanks again for arranging everything. I know the funeral will be a wonderful one. The Lord's presence will ensure a pleasant and comforting event. I love you all.

Bye—see all of you later.
Sebastian Yeo, 26.8.98

Wow! Sebastian was forgiven totally and completely! He faced the end of his life with a heavenly hope!

Can you trust the promises of God in the Bible?

Can you expect that prayer will work?

Can you be sure of forgiveness?

Can good come out of evil?

Can your hurts become halos? Your scars change to stars?

Absolutely!

TEN COMMANDMENTS FOR HURTING HEARTS

Like the Ten Commandments in the Old Testament, my Ten Commandments for Hurting Hearts have some *shalls* and *shall nots*. There are five *don'ts* and five *dos* that are fundamental principles of healing therapy for hurting hearts.

Set up these five don'ts and five dos like fence bars around your hurt to shield your wounded spirit in its fragile and vulnerable state.

FIVE DON'TS

1. Whatever you do, don't make a swift, irreversibly negative decision when you take the hit.

You're hurt. You're not at your strongest. You may, in fact, be at your weakest. You are simply not in the best condition to make any serious moves at all. Certainly you must not make negative decisions when you are at your weakest or at your worst! Every wartime fighter pilot has been taught: If you take

John Newton suffered from the internal anguish of his own sinful behavior and involvement in the sordid traffic of human slavery. He found salvation from his shame and wrote these words:

AMAZING GRACE!
HOW SWEET THE SOUND

Amazing grace! How sweet the sound, that saved a wretch like me! I once was lost but now am found, was blind but now I see.

'Twas grace that taught my heart to fear, and grace my fears relieved; how precious did that grace appear the hour I first believed!

Through many dangers, toils, and snares, I have already come; 'tis grace hath brought me safe thus far, and grace will lead me home.

The Lord has promised good to me, His word my hope secures; He will my shield and portion be as long as life endures.

—JOHN NEWTON (1725–1807)

a hit, don't make a move. Don't touch anything. Just sit tight, and *think!*

Do nothing? Check the damage, of course, if you are losing blood. Stop the bleeding—now! Then pull yourself together. You can. You must do nothing! Take a deep breath! Sit tight and *think! think!* Positively!

2. Don't emotionalize the issue.

Of course, your emotions will threaten to overwhelm you! Anger, guilt, fear, shame, loss of self-esteem, resentment, depression—any or all of these emotions—will naturally and normally flow through your pain.

But don't surrender leadership of your thinking to these feelings. You simply cannot and must not trust these seductive spirits. Of course you can and should release these emotions. Have a good cry. Verbalize your fragile feelings. Whatever you do, don't internalize the grief or anger and hypocritically pretend you're "fine"! Release these negative emotions to your O.E.F. (One Essential Friend), your pastor, or your counselor. Be honest. Don't pretend, repress, or fake the painful feelings!

But don't emotionalize—draw judgmental

conclusions from these feelings, like "I'm a horrible sinner" or "I'm so dumb." Of all the times in your life, this is the time to lead with your head, not with your wounded, broken, bleeding heart.

3. Don't personalize the pain.

Maybe you should take the hurt personally, but not now. There'll be time for that later, if that is appropriate. But the grave danger is to take the hurt personally when you should not. Hundreds of times I've heard, "He (she) takes it personally but shouldn't."

The company discharged you? The love of your life has cut you off and out? Your great challenge is to follow your smart head, not your smarting heart. For you are a good person, and good people are so sincere they'll blame themselves, not others. They'll fault their shortcomings, whereas the cause may be other factors, forces, or faces. In a fast-moving world—where cultures are changing, economic markets are shifting, relationships are on the move, and values are being revised—*be careful.* Be slow to take the hurt personally. *Because it's in your heart doesn't mean you should take it on your shoulders.*

Be slow to take the blame, but be quick to take aim. Resight your goals. Take a fresh mental picture of your dreams.

4. Don't make matters worse than they are.

The first reaction to many hurtful experiences is the compulsion to give in to the pain—and make it worse than it is! So don't exaggerate the seriousness of it all.

One of my Pastoral Heroes of History is Bishop Phillips Brooks. A life-size bronze statue of this great Episcopal priest stands outside his prominent church in downtown Boston, Massachusetts. He is best known as the author of "O Little Town of Bethlehem," which he wrote one Christmas Eve, sitting alone on the shepherds' hills outside Bethlehem, where he was suffering from a nervous breakdown. (He would recover, return to America, and become one of the greatest pastors in America's history.)

One morning a distraught parishioner telephoned Phillips Brooks. This emotionally devastated man was one of Boston's most prestigious professionals. "Pastor, have you seen the morning paper? I'm ruined!" Then he told the story to Bishop Brooks.

When he finished, the pastor said, "Well, first, I didn't read the morning paper. I never do. More than half the people in the town never do. They only read the late afternoon paper.

"Second, of the people who get the paper, only a fraction will read this section.

"Third, the people who read it will be your friends or your enemies. Don't worry about your enemies; they're not on your side anyway. And the friends who read it? The wise and thoughtful people in this group won't believe it. They'll be on the line to defend you before you know it! Yes, in your heart you have been hurt by this. But ruined?! No way!"

5. Don't surrender leadership of your life to negative facts, negative faces, negative fears—or a negative faith.

Negative faith?! Yes, faith can be positive or negative. Negative faith is believing that God is angry with you. Negative faith is assuming you are being punished for your sins. Reject this destructive notion. God takes no pleasure in seeing you suffer.

God loves you and is way ahead of you in planning and preparing to save and strengthen you!

Review and rehearse these five don'ts; then move on to the five dos.

FIVE DOS

1. Do check your value system.

I was walking to my car, parked in a large parking structure, when I passed a white Rolls Royce convertible parked near my car. Standing next to the door on the passenger's side was an elegantly dressed older woman. Next to her stood a well-groomed male companion.

Freeze-framed in my memory I see her now. Her left hand flashed a huge diamond, rectangular cut, well over one-half inch long and over one-quarter inch wide. Her right hand stretched out to the side of her luxury car door. Her second finger pointed to, and almost touched, a black scratch that was probably two inches long. Her angry voice was loud and ugly as she discovered the fresh mark. "Life is hell, isn't it!" she scowled.

Is this your value system? Or is your value

system closer to that of an Englishman I knew?

In the last half of the twentieth century, one literary person stands out in my experience. His name is Malcolm Muggeridge. Remember him and how he became a believer when he met Mother Teresa? At his peak, his name and face were tagged as more recognizable in London than Queen Elizabeth's.

I remember my last visit with him in his tiny country place in Sussex, England. His small living room had space for only four chairs (none of them matched!) and a small coffee table, scratched and scarred but sturdy. His wife brought out tea. None of the cups or saucers matched. They were chipped and faded in color.

"What good tea!" I said honestly and sincerely.

His eyes twinkled. We talked. We laughed. We had a wonderful, entertaining, and stimulating time together. What fun and fellowship we had, talking mostly about history—and Jesus Christ.

I left there thinking the little old cottage could burn down and Muggeridge wouldn't be hurt much. I sensed he could experience health conditions that could claim his life, and he'd be prepared to pass on with a smile in his soul.

So what are your values? Are you a materialist? a narcissist? a social climber? a power-club joiner? Are you a purely secular, sensual, sexual creature without noble spiritual and honorable moral values? I think not, or you would not be reading this book. But check, double check, then recheck your value system.

Remember, the Ten Commandments delivered to the people of Israel by Moses are ten rules given by God to protect us from really hurting ourselves.

Our value system determines our destiny. Years ago, when I first discovered psychology in Hope College, I was so excited. I wanted to be a minister. For a brief time I wondered if I could help more people by becoming a psychiatrist. I shared my concerns with my professor, who said, "Well, keep one thing in mind, Bob. Psychologists and psychiatrists are called to operate under a system of ethics that restricts them from imposing their value systems on their patients. You'd probably be more liberated if you'd become a minister. I'm sure that many human problems are rooted in faulty value systems, and you'd be free to get to these roots." That settled my career commitment!

2. Do listen to the caring voices you have never heard before.

Be open to the possibility that there is a living, loving God. God may be trying to connect with you to help you with a burst of faith that you have never before been willing to consider as a reality. There are so many worlds within worlds, and the best and brightest of us have never been exposed to many of the realities of this spiritual universe.

Whoever you are, wherever you are, whatever you are—believer, atheist, or agnostic—I must share what I truly believe. There is a God "out there," and there is a God inside you too! Since your birth this Eternal Super Spirit called God has made and is making millions of moves to connect with your spirit.

Look and listen to the positive ideas, moods, emotions, impulses, memories, and mental assumptions that are constantly entering your consciousness. Whatever stimulates your sense of aliveness could well be a message from God. Or the aliveness could be the very presence of God within you!

The Bible claims to present the voice and word of God to humans on planet earth. Here we read: “Lo, I am with you always” (Matthew 28:20). God can inspire and inject ideas into your mind or feelings into your heart.

With six billion humans on earth, God has six billion possible humans to use in his network of communicating to other persons. So long as we can see, hear, notice, and be influenced (however slightly) by another human, we may be getting a message from the God who knows all, cares compassionately, and is making connections to our hearts, minds, and spirits, even if we don’t attribute any life or credit to Him. Be open to see and hear God in anything or anyone.

3. Do see your hurt as a process, not as an event.

The hurt has not happened; it is happen*ing*. The outline of this painful scene will change shape as the hours, days, weeks, months, and years unfold. Therefore, it is all important for you to understand that your reaction, more than anything else, will shape the force and the face of this initial pain that hits you.

That's why positive affirmations are all-important. Try thinking, *I can diminish the negative impact of this hurt on my life*. Or, *I can change my hurt until it changes from an enemy into a helpful friend.*

Change is inevitable. You change. The world around you changes. Your circle of acquaintances and friends changes.

> *Your hurt is a mountain on the move!*

Your perspective of the whole painful experience will also change! Your needs will change. Your desires will change. It is absolutely certain that your perception of the hurt is in a process that is on the move! Believe that!

Remember Jesus' promise: "If you have faith as a mustard seed, your mountain will *move,* and nothing will be impossible for you" (Matthew 17:20, author's paraphrase).

4. Do ask the question, What's the worst that can happen?

Believe that, with all your positive-thinking faith, you'll be able to handle the worst!

For the worst has been faced by thousands, perhaps millions, of other positive-thinking human beings before you. They were not overwhelmed by this "worst," and often they overwhelmed the worst when it hit. So will you if the worst really happens, only to collide with a spiritual power inside you!

"God sends no more hurt than we can bear" is the testimony of millions of persons who have experienced horrific hurts.

But what humans cannot handle is a mystery. So take your pain and fear out of the unreliable realm of negative fantasy and exaggerated imagination by asking the question, What's the worst that can happen? Face this prospect, for you as a God-inspired human are more than a match for the worst! You can, after all, face death, as we all surely will one day, and we're ready for that because our Leader and Lord, Jesus Christ, showed us how to get through that valley!

5. Do think positively about the possibilities that lie ahead.

How do you do this? Look at what you have left, never at what you have lost. What's left for you? Family? Friends? Freedom to make new moves in relationships, in career choices, in asset management? Listen. You might hear an inner voice saying, "Come. It's time to move on."

Rehearse these five don'ts and five dos, and let your hurts lead you to higher ground. Here you will see others who need help and encouragement. You have something to give. Now more than ever!

The secret of success, remind yourself, is to find a hurt and heal it. Find a need and fill it. Look around you in your community, your church, your city or village and see the possibilities of becoming kindness incarnate.

Now you will be focused on tomorrow with its possibilities instead of focused on yesterday and today with its pain.

Now you will get a new dream. You'll become a goal-setting, goal-managed, and dream-driven person!

And this, more than anything else, will be the beginning of turning your hurt into a halo!

"What better way to test a professional athlete than through his body? I could easily have been destroyed when I was paralyzed out on the football field. I was weak and vulnerable, but 2 Corinthians 12:9 says, 'And He said to me, "My grace is sufficient for you, for My strength is made perfect in weakness." ' He is with us when we break, and He can help make us whole."

—DENNIS BYRD
FORMER NEW YORK JETS
DEFENSIVE END AND QUADRIPLEGIC

5

HURTS NEVER LEAVE YOU WHERE THEY FIND YOU!

YES, YOU'RE ON A TRIP CALLED LIFE. Did you choose this tour? Did you buy this ticket? "Of course not!" you answer. That answer is both right and wrong.

- You chose to drive; you didn't choose to have that accident.
- You chose to marry for love; you did not choose to be betrayed.
- Your spouse died. (This trip you're on—grief—you didn't choose it! Or did you?)

Wait a minute. This hurt you're experiencing is the cost you pay for the happiness you chose. Life is a toll road. Everything that's nice has its price.

"My hearing is going. It's hard to grow old," one man said to me with a negative overtone. I admonished him (I think gently but honestly) with this short sermon: "Grow-

Every adversity is an adventure.
Every pain is a pilgrimage.
Every trial is a trail.
Every problem is a path.
Every load is a road.
Every hurt is on the move.
It's leading you somewhere.
Where is it taking you?

ing old is the price we pay for not dying young."

Now you're on an adventure. A pilgrimage. A trip and a tour through a land where you've never traveled before. Some decision you made somewhere, sometime, put you on this path, and you are now surprised at the toll gate. You chose the path, not knowing the price.

Warning! Don't make the impertinent, unintelligent, and cynical assumption that the price is too high.

> *"Growing old is the price we pay for not dying young."*

The well-known saying "It's better to have loved and lost, than never to have loved at all" is all too true.

Yes, the price you have to pay might seem high. But recall all the pleasures, satisfactions, and benefits, and you'll have a rebirth of positive possibility thinking. Your heart will move from pain to praise.

Pay the toll and thank God for the trip you've had! Alicia Blake did just that.

Alicia Blake, and her husband, Don, were

charter members of the new church my wife and I started in 1955.

One afternoon there was an unexpected knock at our front door. My wife, Arvella, answered and saw Alicia. "Alicia! Come in!" Arvella beamed.

The always-smiling Alicia wasn't smiling. "No, I can't stay, dear," she said. "I have just come from the hospital, where Don died from a sudden heart attack. Just this morning we had a wonderful breakfast! We never knew there was a thing wrong."

"Oh, no, Alicia! Please, sit down," Arvella offered. "Bob should be home very soon."

"No, I'll be all right, Arvella." She explained, "I had to stop and tell you and Bob. But now I've got to go home and do the hardest thing first. And that's to sit in his favorite chair! If I can do that, then I'll be able to go on and get on."

Alicia went on to use all of her "free time" as a widow working in the church as a number-one volunteer. Alicia Blake helped make the Crystal Cathedral in Garden Grove, California, the largest congregation of any faith in the world. Millions visit these Sunday services every week—sitting in their cars in the drive-in section, or in pews under the glass ceiling, or in overflow rooms, or watching on television in homes, hotels, and hospitals around the world in over two hundred countries.

Pee Wee Kirkland[1] was destined to be one of the great basketball stars of the 1970s. His name should be a household name now, like that of Michael Jordan or Isaiah Thomas. Sportswriters still consider him to be one of the best point guards to come out of Harlem.

The Chicago Bulls snapped him out of the NBA draft. He held incredible promise. But rather than enjoying a starring role on the basketball court, Pee Wee Kirkland spent eleven of the next eighteen years behind bars in federal penitentiaries, convicted of selling drugs and evading taxes.

Yet in his hurt he found himself. "I realized how wrong I was and I knew I could do better," he says. "I knew God expected better things from me."

Upon his release from prison, Pee Wee followed up on his commitment to improve himself and to make a difference. He started the School of Skillz, a basketball program for Harlem kids at the Central Baptist Church in Harlem, New York. Using his hurt as a lesson

> *Your hurt can change you from a zero to a hero.*

tool, Pee Wee has become a role model for many kids in the inner city.

Today he is the basketball coach for Dwight School, an exclusive prep school in New York. There he focuses on building not only a great basketball program, but also helping kids know what it means to have a dream and the desire to work for it.

Wow! Look where Pee Wee Kirkland's hurt led him.

He was a somebody.
Then a nobody.
He was worth a lot.
Then he was worth nothing.
But he rebuilt!

Today Pee Wee Kirkland is one of the most loved and respected coaches in America.

He went from a zero to a hero!

How You Handle Hurt Can Make Headlines!

I know I'll never forget one infamous game. As a lifelong Dodger fan, I avidly cheered for the Los Angeles baseball team under the leadership of my good friend Tommy Lasorda. Like most teams, they have had their ups and downs, good seasons and bad ones. But one year that stands out in history is 1988.

The Dodgers were playing phenomenally. They had won the pennant and were heading into the World Series against the Oakland A's. One of L.A.'s best players was Kirk Gibson, who exemplified a winning spirit for the team. As he told me in an interview on the *Hour of Power*, "We developed this vision that we were going to be the world champions. We imprinted it on our minds; we didn't take no for an answer."

But in winning the pennant, Gibson played so intensely that he injured both legs. As the Dodgers walked out for the opening game of the World Series, Gibson was sidelined, out of uniform. He sat in the clubhouse and listened to Dodger announcer Vince Scully repeat, "Gibson will not be playing tonight. He's not even in the dugout."

The game went on without him. Here's how Gibson recalls what happened next.

"I kept visualizing winning the game. One

shot. One at bat. It was all I could give, my only chance to contribute. It was the end of the eighth inning, Oakland led 4-3. Going into the ninth, we were running out of players. I heard Scully announce, 'Looking to the ninth for the Dodgers will be Scosa, Hamilton, Griffin, followed by the pitcher.' *The pitcher?"*

The pitcher was not known as a good hitter—and so Gibson made up his mind. He called Tommy Lasorda from the clubhouse and said, "Put me in for the pitcher."

"One of the things I had told myself was, 'Even though I'm injured, when I walk on that field at Dodger Stadium and I hear that crowd, because they're counting on me, I won't hurt anymore. I'm gonna go up and do my job.' And crazy enough, I went out there; the crowd went nuts; and it didn't hurt. I looked at the pitcher and said under my breath, 'You don't know what you've got coming. We're going to win this game, and I'm gonna win it for us.' "

The scene was played out in front of millions of television spectators. Commentators still recall today with awed fascination how out of the dugout came a severely limping Gibson. He winced with each step toward home plate. Despite his obvious pain, his eyes were on fire. He bravely took the first pitch from relief pitcher Dennis Eckersly. Strike one! The second pitch came past. Strike two! The pitcher had struck out two of the previous batters and had walked only one. The tying run was at first base. Gibson would become the winning run.

"I was in emergency mode. I fought and fought and fought until I got up to three balls and two strikes. One more strike and I was out. Now the scouts had told me if Dennis Eckersly got me to three balls and two strikes, he would throw me a certain type of pitch called a backdoor slider. So I stepped out of the batter's box and said to myself, 'Partner, as sure as I'm standing here, I'm going to see a backdoor slider.' I stepped back into the box, and guess what he threw me?"

Gibson connected with the backdoor slider and hit the home run! The stadium erupted. The Dodgers won the game. The off-balance gait of Gibson as he hobbled around the bases with his arms in the air has been replayed in sports highlights over and over. He made the most triumphant lap of his life in the most important game of his life when he was hurt the most! The Oakland A's never recovered, and the Dodgers went on to win the World Series Championship.

Kirk Gibson could have quit and opted not to try. But it was in his adversity that the world witnessed what resolute drive he had. He became a hero to millions of sports fans around the world. That's where his hurt took him.

"I believe that God created this wonderful world and put us here to enjoy it, and to do the best we can do," Kirk said to me. "But in our lives, we will experience adversity. If you have faith, you have someplace to turn, and somebody to help you through that time of need. In that process, you will become a better person. Your faith becomes stronger, and it prepares you to help others in their time of need by sharing your faith with them. That's what it's all about. When you're down, I'm going to pick you up. And when I'm down, you're going to pick me up, or you're not on my team."

That's Kirk Gibson's philosophy and mine too. You—and no one else but you—will determine the direction! I'm positive that there's a possibility in every adversity!

Romans 8:28—"All things work together

for good to those who love God"—could be the single most important Bible verse in your life. Every problem and pain is pregnant with positive possibilities in the mind of a positive thinker! This never, never fails!

> *Your hurt may still be alive tomorrow . . . but it will be changed. Your hurt will change because your attitude and your perception are changing.*

Yes, the hurt is on the move. Sometime, somehow, someway, the hurt you knew will no longer be what it was when it first hit you.

And then what will you have?

A scar! That's when every hurt is healed!

Turn Your Scars into Stars

The Bible makes an astonishing promise—that out of your weakness shall come strength (Hebrews 11:34).

That is like saying that where a bone was broken, it was knit, welded, and healed; and it became stronger there than at any other point.

It is like saying that where the flesh was

cut and the tissue healed, the skin mended and a scar formed; and that scar became tougher than at any other point on the surface of the body.

Some years ago in the Netherlands, a guide said to me as we walked across the dike, "See the huge concrete plug? That is where we had a leak one time. The sea rushed in and many people perished, but we plugged it with concrete, reinforced it with steel, and it will never break there again."

"Where you are weak, there you will be made strong."

Once when I was making a hospital call, a doctor said to me as he pointed to a nurse walking down the hallway, "She is the best nurse we have. How she works. She is so dedicated." Then, as an afterthought he said, "That is because when she was a teenager she spent ten months on her back in this hospital."

You can turn your scars into stars! Your hurts can be turned into halos! Yes, out of your weakness shall come strength.

There is a key principle here: If you want to live an emotionally healthy and happy life, you have to know how to handle the hurts that come.

Several forms of hurts may strike. First, there is such a thing as being hurt by your friends. Second, we all know what it is like, I suppose, to be hurt by an enemy.

There is also a third type of hurt, the wound that you inflict upon yourself and later hate yourself for.

Hurts inflicted by friends, enemies, and yourself are painful, but there are also hurts that you can only say *life* threw at you. For instance, the bridge collapsed, and you got hurt. You can't pin blame on anyone, not even yourself; at a time like that, it is always tempting to blame God. Be careful! The odds are that some human being made a mistake, and that is why the accident happened.

Finally, there are hurts that God causes. A loved one is taken home. God took him (or her), and you are hurt. Yet when you married, God never promised how long you could have each other; it was simply for better or for worse, till death do you part. Your time with your loved one might have been a day, a week, a month, perhaps a year, maybe even ten years. God made no promises.

The advice from the book of Hebrews is

right; you can turn your weakness into strength. But how do you do it?

Here are four key principles to keep your hurt from becoming what I call an ugly scar. These four points will minimize the scar tissue and let it heal. With these four principles, your scar can become a star:

- Don't curse your hurt!
- Don't rehearse your hurt!
- Don't nurse your hurt!
- Disperse your hurt! (I will show you how.)
- Reverse your hurt! Turn it inside out. The hurt will become a halo. The scar will become a star.

FOUR PRINCIPLES TO TURN SCARS INTO STARS

1. DON'T CURSE YOUR HURT!

I hear it all the time: "See her," they say, "she has been drinking a lot since she lost her husband."

Or they point to him and say, "You know, he has been going downhill ever since his boy died."

Or they say, "He dropped out of high

Turn your hurts inside out
And . . .
Turn the problem into a project,
the enemy into a friend,
the hurt into a halo,
the scar into a star.

school when he was a senior because he didn't make the football team. That did it."

Or they point to her and say, "I think I'm going to have to let her go; she is just not doing her work. Ever since she didn't get the promotion, she hasn't been much good to the company."

There are many ways to curse our hurts. Curse them, and you become bitter. Anytime somebody is hurt, he or she becomes either a bitter person or a better person.

Don't curse your hurts. It's like picking at a scab. The more you pick it, the more it bleeds and the more scarring there will be. What's needed is the healing salve of positive affirmations, not negative, nasty words.

2. DON'T REHEARSE OR NURSE YOUR HURT!

I remember a lady who called my office, a dear friend of mine whose husband had passed away some years ago. How I wished the poor, dear soul had come to me sooner, one and a half years ago, or at least one year ago. She waited so long, too long, crying inside alone, killing herself with grief.

She had been rehearsing how it all happened! How he was acting eight weeks before he had the heart attack, six weeks before, four weeks before, and three weeks before. Then she recalled what he did the week before the attack and, finally, the fatal morning. She had rehearsed the scene over and over again in her mind.

After she told me all this, she opened her large purse and got out her billfold. "I have something here that I always carry with me. I wanted to know just why he died. So I asked the doctor, couldn't they have tried electric shock to start the heart, or opened it and massaged it, or something?"

The doctor had given this woman a very technical, clinical definition of how her husband died. She said, "I copied it down on this piece of paper, and I carry it with me all the time."

I don't remember it exactly, but it was something to this effect: "Your husband's condition started because of an inner problem in the arteries, which became clogged, then blood clots formed, and finally one of the large clots got so large it closed off the whole passage so that the blood could no longer flow into the heart. When that happened, the valve closed off and an enormous pain came. The lungs were no longer able to expand, and then he died from a lack of oxygen."

I cried with her as I prayed with her, and God performed a healing there in my study. I said to her, "Now, I want to say one final thing before you leave. One last piece of advice."

"Sure, Reverend, anything you say."

"I want you to take that piece of paper, and I want you to tear it up and throw it away. Don't ever look at it again."

She said, "Really? Do you think that is what I should do?"

"I know that is what you should do."

"Okay, Reverend, I'll do that." And she did. The next time I saw her, a new sparkle was back in her personality.

If you nurse and rehearse your hurt, you will finally develop what psychologists call a neurosis—an abnormal attention to a compulsive emotion, which will make you worse, not better.

Instead of nursing your hurts, disperse them.

3. DISPERSE YOUR HURT!

You probably can't help it when the hurt comes, but you can help it if the hurt lasts.

Through the power of God and through the power of prayer, you can handle any hurt. I know this is true. But you have to pray the right way.

A friend was having a problem with a competitor, and he was experiencing all kinds of negative emotions. I suggested he pray about it.

"What do I pray?" he asked. "Do I pray that the guy will succeed?"

"Well, I don't know. Just pray that God will tell you what to pray. Ask God what to pray for," I responded.

A week later, my friend told me, "I woke up at two o'clock in the morning, and I had the prayer."

"What was it?"

He told me this was the prayer:

Dear God, make that person into exactly the person you want him to be and cause his business to develop just the way you would like to see it develop. Amen.

My friend continued, "That just completely cured me. Now, if that guy's business succeeds, I can't possibly be angry about it. I

> *You can be sure of one thing—the hurt you know today wants to move and leave you. Please let it go!*

know God wants it to grow." He was very sincere.

If you have a hurt and have prayed about it, but your prayer hasn't helped, then you may have prayed the wrong prayer. Instead, start by asking God what you ought to pray about.

To really get rid of your hurt, begin by looking deep into yourself. Somehow you have to find at what point you were at fault. If you have a problem with someone, I am sure it is not 100 percent the other person's fault. The hardest and the most healing word in the Bible is the word *repent*. That may be what you need to do.

You can disperse your hurts if your relationship with God is right.

Are you suffering from a hurt that is self-inflicted? Do you hate yourself for what you have done? Maybe you are cheating on your wife, or your wife is cheating on you. Maybe you are stealing from your employer, or you are dishonest and you hate like Hades the person you see in the mirror.

Oh, God, you say, *if there were just some way to tear out the black page and start over again!*

There is! You can disperse your hurt!

Say, *Jesus Christ, take me, cleanse me, forgive me. God, if you forgive me, I will be able to live with myself.*

Start over fresh and clean!

How do you handle your hurts? Don't curse them, don't rehearse them and nurse them, but disperse them, and, finally, reverse your hurts.

4. REVERSE YOUR HURT!

The more I read about great people and the more I meet them, the more I am convinced of one thing: there is no great person alive who has not been hurt deeply.

Let's look at the stories of two people who have followed these four principles to turn their scars into stars: Dr. Dan Poling and the woman who became our Helping Hand project director.

They Have Turned Their Scars into Stars

When I was a young pastor, I was invited to preach in the Marble Collegiate Church in New York City. Dr. Norman Vincent Peale was the senior pastor of that church, but at that time the evening preacher was Dr. Daniel A. Poling. I didn't know Dr. Poling, and when I came to preach in that church I didn't have my pulpit robe with me. (They hadn't asked me to bring a pulpit robe on a five-hour flight, where it can get really wrinkled.) So they looked for one that would fit. They reached into the closet and said, *"Here, Dr. Dan's should fit you."*

I slipped into it. I fastened the buttons all the way down, but one button came off. I slipped it into my pants pocket. Later that week I mailed it back east with a letter to Dr. Dan Poling. "My apologies, sir, but here is a button off your robe."

I got a letter back that you wouldn't believe. It was fantastic! Remember that I was an unknown youth, just a few years away from the Iowa farm. Dr. Poling wrote, "The loss of a button is a cheap price to pay for the honor of having you wear my robe, good sir."

Later on I learned the secret of Dr. Poling's greatness. In World War I he was a chaplain. He ran between trenches that were only a hundred yards apart. A hail of bullets went around him and soldiers fell dead, yet he came out alive.

In another instance he was one of four men carrying a litter that held a German prisoner with a mangled leg. A shell exploded in the mud around him.

All others were blown to pieces, but Dan Poling lived through it.

Years later, he faced an incredible challenge with his son, Clark, a teenager in a private school located out of the city. Clark sent a telegram saying, "Dad, I am coming home this weekend. I want to see you alone. Meet me at the depot."

Dr. Dan met his teenage boy at the depot, wondering what kind of trouble his son was in. Together they went to Dr. Poling's office at the Marble Collegiate Church. When the boy noticed there was no lock, he took a chair and put it under the doorknob so nobody would interrupt their conversation.

"By this time," Dr. Dan said later, "I was

really trembling inside. I sat behind my desk, and my boy came and pulled up a chair next to mine and then put his elbows on top of my desk. He put his chin in his hands and just looked.

"Now," the father continued, "I have made many mistakes in my life, but I didn't make a mistake here by asking what was wrong . . . I just waited.

"Finally, my boy looked at me and said, 'Dad, tell me, what do you know about God?'

"I looked back at him and said, 'What do I know about God? Very little, my son, very little. But enough to change my whole life!'

"The boy looked back and said, 'That's good enough, that's good enough. I think I'll be a preacher like you when I grow up.' And he did. He graduated from seminary, married, and had a beautiful baby."

Then, on December 7, 1941, the bombs fell on Pearl Harbor. Clark came to his dad and said, "Dad, I'm going to enlist as a chaplain. The only problem is, Dad, I think that is taking the easy way out."

Dr. Dan looked at his son and said, "Don't you say that, Son. I will have you know that in the First World War, the most dangerous post you could have was the post of chaplain. On a percentage basis more chaplains died in the First World War than infantrymen—one out of ninety-three, to be specific. If you become a chaplain, you may have your chance to die, Clark."

Clark became a chaplain. His father was in London when he heard the news that the S.S. Dorchester, a troop ship with over nine hundred on board, was torpedoed off Greenland, and there were only a handful of survivors. The rest went down with the ship.

One of the survivors said that the last scene, as the bow of the ship was about to slip beneath the cold waters, was the sight of four chaplains standing together on the bow. Each one was unstrapping his own life preserver and handing it to a private who jumped into the water and was saved.

Then, having given their life preservers away, the four chaplains—two Protestants, a Catholic, and a Jew—all went down. One of these four was Clark Poling.

Since that time, Dr. Dan's heart became so big, he wanted to take in every boy alive on planet earth. He wanted to be Dad to everybody.

Dan Poling turned his scars into stars. So

did the volunteer who directed our Helping Hands project.

A while back I stepped out of my office to tell my secretary something. Just then the elevator doors opened, and there was this young mother with a little girl pulling at her skirt. The mother looked busy, rushed, and even a little harassed.

I said to my secretary, "Who is she? What is she doing here at this time of day?"

My secretary reminded me that she was now in charge of our Helping Hand project.

This young woman was spending hours and hours at our church. Doing what? Collecting tin cans full of soup and beans. People call into our telephone counseling center, NEW HOPE, twenty-four hours a day.

The Crystal Cathedral is the first church in the United States to operate a twenty-four-hour live telephone counseling program, operated solely by members of the church. People call and tell us they have nothing. We have a policy that we won't give money to people. If they have no food, we will supply them with groceries.

Now this young mother, who herself was so busy, was devoting hours every week to manage this whole operation. Only a few people knew how much work and time were involved.

I commented on that, and my secretary said, "You remember when she wrote you a letter that really moved you and impressed you? I've saved it. Let me get it." The letter read:

Dear Dr. Schuller:

I can't begin to thank you for your congregation. What wonderful Christians they are. My husband has been flat on his back in bed for months and can't work. I had a baby who became sick, and I couldn't work.

The church heard about it and the ladies came and brought us breakfast, dinner, and supper. They did this week after week, day after day. How can I ever repay you? How can I ever repay them?

She found a way.

Again and again, if I look at a great person I think, *Somewhere that person was hurt.*

You can turn your hurt into a halo. You can turn your scar into a star! That's what one creative Iranian did.

I have toured royal palaces around the

> *Let a hopeful heart —not a hurting heart— lead you.*

world, but the Royal Palace in Tehran, Iran, is something else! There isn't anything like it, to my knowledge, anywhere in the world.

You step into the Royal Palace, and the grand entrance is resplendent with glittering, sparkling glass. For a moment you think that the domed ceilings, side walls, and columns are all covered with diamonds . . . until you realize that these are not diamonds or cut glass; they are small pieces of mirrors. The edges of a myriad of little mirrors reflect the light, throwing out the colors of the rainbow! A mosaic of mirrors!

Spectacular!

You'll never believe how this happened. When the Royal Palace was planned, the architects sent an order to Paris for mirrors to cover the entrance walls. The mirrors finally arrived in their crates. When they took the crates apart, all the broken pieces fell out! They were all smashed in travel! They were going to junk them all when one creative man said, "No, maybe it will be more beautiful because the mirrors are broken."

So he took some of the larger pieces and smashed them, and then he took all the little pieces and fitted them together like an abstract mosaic. If you see it, you will note that it is an enormous distortion in reflections, and it sparkles with diamondlike rainbow colors.

Broken to be more beautiful!

Do you have a hurt?

If you do, turn it over to God, and He will turn it inside out.

He will reverse it, and it will become a star instead of a scar in your crown!

"Why do bad things happen to good people?" is the wrong question. For there is no answer.

The right question is, "What happens to good people when bad things happen to them?"

The answer? They always become better people!

6
Are You Making It Hard for People to Help You?

A FEW MONTHS AGO my wife and I were sitting in a hotel breakfast room when a man came in with his two small sons and sat at the adjoining table.

"What did you do with your socks?" the father asked one of his sons. The tone hinted of an appropriate parental rebuke. The dialogue continued. I couldn't hear the conversation, but then the father spoke, not softly, but firmly, "Are you making it hard for people to help you?!"

I returned to my room to continue the writing of this book, and the question haunted me. Do hurting people make it hard for people to help them? If so, do they know it? And if so, why would hurting people hurt the people who are trying to help them?

Remember the lady in Hawaii who said to me, "The hurt that pained me the most through it all was not what he did to me so much as having to see what he was doing to himself. It hurts so badly to see someone you love hurting himself and refusing all efforts to rescue him from a path that leads to shame and ruin?"

The deeper question is, Why do people reject, resist, or fail to recognize all the help that's available?

In a summary sentence, here's my answer to that crucial question: The wounded heart may instinctively yield to overwhelming negative emotions. And that's where we consciously, or unconsciously, make it extremely difficult for people to help us.

Control . . . Control . . . Control . . .

Probably nothing is more difficult for strong persons than to admit and accept the helplessness that overwhelms them strangely and suddenly in the dark times. Mature, responsible, and intelligent persons have developed deep character traits, which compel them to personal responsibility and high accountability. When faced with a horrific hurt, where they are for all practical purposes helpless, they are put in a position where they may have to admit that they are no longer able to handle everything all by themselves.

There are times for each of us when we are no longer in control. This is a devastating emotional experience we have never encountered before! The last thing we want to do is admit that we are helpless and are dealing with a problem that is beyond our control.

That is why Alcoholics Anonymous can provide real help to helpless cases—but not until that person can break free from denial. This cannot and will not happen until the addict confesses, "I have a problem and I cannot handle it. Only with the help of a higher power can I overcome my addiction."

What drives this denial?

The human ego has an almost infinite ability to rationalize. People don't want to admit they need help. But hurting hearts will never find health and healing until they admit, with authentic humility, their helplessness.

"I need help. I can never make it alone and on my own."

My wife learned this after her surgery. "The most difficult thing about my open heart surgery," she said, "was this sense of helplessness. I could not raise my own head above the pillow. People had to slip their hands behind my head and lift it so I could have a sip of water. Never before was I so dependent upon the help of others. Helplessness was one thing I was not prepared to have to accept."

A recent interview guest at the Crystal Cathedral was a young man from southern California named Scott McClung. Scott belongs to a strong Christian family and has the financial resources for an amazing ministry. Together with his father, Scott provides certified marine expeditions on their boat, which takes kids out to the Channel Islands of California and down to the Sea of Cortez in Mexico. There the kids not only learn about God, but also experience His creation through kayaking, diving, and educational activities in and out of the water.

In an effort to expand this ministry, the McClungs recently built a second boat in Florida, a beautiful vessel that would sleep 150 kids. Father, son, and crew were in the process of bringing the ship back to California when something beyond their control went terribly wrong. In Scott's own words:

"We had crossed the Gulf of Mexico, and the evening before we pulled into Cozumel, we ran across a wonderful example of God's creation—a pod of about a hundred whale sharks. We dove with them and filmed them underwater. It was an awesome experience. But then we experienced some mechanical difficulty, which forced us to pull into Cozumel.

"As required, we declared our cash and firearms to the local federal prosecutor, who had come out to the boat with his agents. He said everything was fine, and he had a Coke, played Foosball with us, and left.

"However, later that night he showed up again, along with two other boats full of navy personnel. They were armed with automatic weapons and took me, my father, and our chief mate into custody. They interrogated us from seven-thirty that night until nine-thirty the next morning. We were separated, roughed around quite a bit, and not allowed any food or water. Most of their questions were about money. Ironically, they finally came up with a bribe figure of ten thousand dollars, which is exactly what we had declared that we had on us. This was money that was to be used for fuel in Costa Rica."

Scott and his father refused to give in to the bribe and subsequently were imprisoned. After nine days, the rogue prosecutor eventually released his father, but Scott was held for a total of forty days. It took a team of attorneys in the United States and in Mexico to secure Scott's freedom as well as the release of the vessel and their belongings. During all of this publicity, an investigation was launched. Through the efforts of the U.S. Ambassador, the U.S. Attorney General, and the President of Human Rights in Mexico, Scott was freed, and with him fifty more innocent people were released from jail!

The period alone in prison gave Scott a lot of time to reflect on God's goodness despite hardships. "God revealed Himself in many different ways," Scott said. "My crew was there for me. If my faith was weak, God had them right there as great examples to not give up."

But Scott also acknowledged that the toughest part of his forty-day incarceration came from his sense of helplessness and lack of control. "Whatever I'm doing, I like to be in control," Scott admitted. "But when you're in jail, you're completely out of control. You have to depend on other people and God for absolutely everything—like where your next meal comes from or whether your window gets opened.

"So it was a great experience to be able to hear God tell me it's okay to be out of control. He calls us all to be little children, not big strong adults who can handle everything. It was a great opportunity to have to be dependent on my crew, my father, and all who prayed for me."

Wow! Scott's story confirms that although we don't like to give up control, sometimes it's the way God really reveals himself. When we have to "let go and let God," miracles happen!

Sometimes negative emotions block the healing process God offers. Anger, depression, and guilt get misdirected to God for allowing the hurt to occur. When you're wounded, these emotions can overwhelm the grief process, making it difficult for the trained eye to see. This is what happened to Karen Johnson.

Karen committed herself to staying home to raise her children in a loving Christian environment until they were well into their school years. When her two daughters and son were in high school, she became director of a Christian crisis pregnancy center. Her ministry to unwed teenagers and unloved mothers was both challenging and fulfilling. She dealt daily with the crises of rape, abuse, and unplanned pregnancies. She offered support to single mothers and counsel to their extended families. She was an expert in family crisis. Yet nothing could prepare her for the irony of the hurt she would face.

When JoAnne, her eldest, was a senior in high school, Karen's perfect world was turned upside down. The stunning blonde teenager was a model child: editor of her school newspaper, gifted writer, and swim team member. She held incredible promise and potential. One month short of her high school graduation, everything changed. JoAnne was raped by a friend in her own living room.

The rape occurred while Karen was out of town and her husband and son were away at a ball game. Mike*, one of JoAnne's

---

*Name has been changed.

swim teammates, had come over to study. The two high schoolers were simply friends. They had enjoyed each other's company before. With no warning Mike simply overpowered JoAnne and raped her.

Two days later, Karen returned home from her trip and found JoAnne curled up in a fetal position on her bed. JoAnne confided the horrible truth to her mother.

As traumatic as the rape had been, the subsequent events seemed even more crushing. There were interviews with the district attorney, humiliating medical exams, and a tape-recorded confession by her rapist. For Karen, the grieving process had begun. And it quickly got stuck in anger.

"I was so angry," remembered Karen, "all I wanted was vengeance."

JoAnne's grieving took on a different expression, one that is common to rape victims. There was an immediate change in her behavior. "I noticed it the very next week," Karen said. "She started to withdraw from her church friends and normal peer group. She started hanging out with a group that partied more.

"That's the effect, I understand now, on

many girls," Karen said. "They have a complete change in behavior. It's as if a switch clicks in their brain that says, *If someone can do that to me, it must mean something about me*."

The summer that followed proved to be one small crisis after another. When fall came, JoAnne selected a small, but strict, Christian college. It was there that she fell apart.

"Every time we talked to her, she was upset. The D.A. was pushing the court case and always calling her. She didn't want her roommates to know about her situation. Her roommates were a wild bunch who wanted to party and take her down to bars in Mexico."

JoAnne decided to quit school, move home, and drop the case against her rapist. It was a move her mother now agrees was the right thing, but during the grieving process, she couldn't get past her anger.

"I was holding on to my anger," Karen said, citing many reasons for doing so. "We had applied to the victims' assistance program to pay for counseling, but the state denied it because she didn't prosecute. Meanwhile I'm thinking, *Mike did this. He gets off scot-free, and my daughter's got all this damage. She has to go to counseling; she has dropped out of school, and we still have to pay her tuition*.

"I clipped and saved newspaper articles about the case and stuck them in a file. I think I was hiding it all away, waiting for God to take vengeance on this kid. He didn't."

Despite Karen's counseling experience, she couldn't recognize her own emotional hang-ups. And she grappled hard with her concept of how God could let her down.

"I had a bi-level view of the universe—that these things happen to other people, not to people who are really dedicated to Christ, really committed to Him. I think I had subconsciously made a deal with God that He would never let anything bad happen to us. I had made the deal, but He hadn't made it with me."

While Karen harbored her anger both at God and at her daughter's attacker, JoAnne's life continued to make quick turns. She met a Navy Seal, fell in love, and got pregnant the weekend he completed his most intensive training. The mother who had counseled pregnant teens now watched helplessly as her own daughter dealt with yet another crisis.

Karen challenged her own assumptions that teenage pregnancy happens only to "bad" girls. She questioned whether her daughter would lean upon her spiritual upbringing and do the right thing for the baby. Karen was rewarded when she did.

JoAnne and her boyfriend, Sean, agreed to keep the baby. On April 30, only 364 days after her rape, JoAnne was married.

In retrospect, Karen can see that she was in a grieving process the whole time. She also acknowledges that it wasn't until she finally gave up her anger—after hearing an especially meaningful sermon in her church—that the healing process was hastened.

Today as she remembers it all, Karen again sounds like the wise and understanding counselor. Only now her words have been truly lived out.

"We are allowed to grieve over death," she said, "but nobody tells you that you can grieve over your daughter's lost future. Or that you can grieve over losing your role as a mother too soon. Or that you can grieve over your daughter losing her virginity in this way. Or that you can grieve over losing the belief that God is going to be there for her."

Karen now sees that God *was* there all the time. "He didn't seem to be solving the problem according to my expectations, without any fallout in JoAnne's life. I sort of expected some kind of magic wand. I realize how naive and wrong that was.

"I can see the big picture that God is at work. He is healing. He is deepening all of us. But coming to that realization requires letting go. I had to let go and let God have His rightful place in my life, in my daughter's life, and now my grandson's life. God is the one in charge, not me."

With fifty years' experience as a full-time professional pastor, I find myself completely convinced that almost unlimited offers of help are extended to any and all good people who are walking the valley of horrific hurt.

God loves you and so do I is the famous line we have used in our global ministry.

Where is God when you are hurting so badly? How can you possibly believe that God loves you when you go through such painful loss? He is in the faces of people who sadly mourn for you. See them mourn, and know that God is telling you that He hurts for you too.

In many marvelous and wonderful ways signals will be sent to your suffering spirit. You may notice a flower blooming. You may hear a bird's song. You may see a toddler running and laughing. You may hear a melody that you have not heard for years. You may feel the touch of sunlight on your cheek, or see its reflection on drops of water on the leaves. An unexpected invitation to breathe calmly will come to your hurting heart.

> *"Just pray for a tough hide and a tender heart."*
> —RUTH BELL GRAHAM

God is alive. Alert. Energetic. Aggressive. God is on the go! Get in that flow. He is sending His spiritual signals into your consciousness. This is God you are experiencing. This is the ultimate healing a human can experience. The very presence of God's spirit is blending into your personality!

These spiritual stimulations can and will come from strange and even foreign faces and places. Be prepared to accept the strong spiritual signals that heaven is sending your way.

Why do people make it hard for good people to help them?

- They have not learned to see these signals of compassion as the presence of God loving them!
- Until they recognize this God who is loving them, they may be unable to dump the negative emotions in their hurting hearts, which are blocking them from accepting help.

Why Do I Refuse Help?

Now ask yourself this same question: Why do I make it hard for people to help me? As you think about that, check the list of negative reactions that might apply to where you are today:

☐ *Angry?* Dump your anger. It will destroy you. Get rid of this emotional enemy.

☐ *Guilt?* Get rid of it. Talk to Jesus Christ, even if you don't know Him. Even if you're not a Christian. Even if you're not a believer. Talk out loud to Him and say: *Jesus Christ, be my Savior. Cleanse me of my guilt. I can't live with it any more. Help me. Amen.*

☐ *Destructive pride?* At its best, pride is a healthy self-esteem, because a low self-esteem will cause you to reject honest help. You will not accept help if you feel unworthy of help. But destructive pride can also be sick egotism. The opposite of a healthy self-respect will keep you from daring to say, "Hey! I need help!"

☐ *Fear of embarrassment?* Do you reject the help that people are offering because you do not want to bring embarrassment on your profession, business, family, or even your faith? I remember a man who said to me, "Everyone has me tagged as one of the strongest members of the church. Pastor, I blew it. I can't let them down by confessing my faults or allowing them to know the hurt that I am going through." (Go back to Chapter 1 in this book, "Welcome to the Human Race.")

Perhaps you think, *I tried it once—or more than once—and the help that was offered then didn't make any difference.* My response is, Why not try again?

- ☐ *Fear of failure?* What if I try it and it doesn't work? What if people come to see me as a wounded person and reject me?
- ☐ *Fear of success?* What if I really am helped and feel indebted to someone? Or what if, deep within me, I fear losing a hurt to which I have developed a negative addiction?
- ☐ *Fear of pain?* "It hurts too much to think about it." My brother, Henry, was a litter bearer in World War II, but he never talked about it. I assumed that he did not see much action, or he'd long forgotten it, or the hurt of it all had healed naturally. Then, fifty years later, I saw the movie *Saving Private Ryan*. World War II came alive on the screen as never before. I shared it with Henry. "I can't see it," he said, adding, "it still hurts too much to think about it."

I know of a woman whose first marriage failed. She had never been able to enjoy a healthy and happy sexual relationship. During counseling she admitted to being sexually abused as a little girl. The psychiatrist who participated with me in the case said, "There is help for people like her, but few cases ever accept help. They have to go back to their childhood in counseling, relive the horrible moment, and begin rebuilding from that point of pain. That is too painful for most adults to handle. The fear of the pain is too heavy."

- ☐ *Genetics?* "It's in my genes. I can't change my DNA." "Its roots are in my nature." "I'll just have to learn to live with it and accept it." "Face it—I'll always be fat, no matter how it hurts."
- ☐ *Fear of intimate exposure?* To accept help could expose a carefully hidden, dark, and dangerous secret. Exposure could lead to divorce, jail, surgery, or dishonorable discharge. Here comes guilt again!

Finally, ask yourself: How can I make it easy for good people to help me?

How Can I Make It Easy for People to Help?

Start with humility and honesty. Those two human values will work miracles in turning anyone with problems into a hurting person who is receptive to the healing touch that reaches out to him.

And that's a win-win relationship! The deepest need is the need to be needed. If you don't want to accept help because you don't want to burden a friend or a stranger, believe me, you aren't burdening him. You'll bless him if you ask for help or accept comfort or compassion from him! Listen to me! In my profession as a pastor, I am complimented when I am asked to help someone who is struggling!

Your humility is a tremendous compliment to your friends, family, and associates. You are saying, in effect, *I'm honestly expressing my pain and hurt to you because:*

- *I trust you.* I see you as a trustworthy person! You are not a gossip! You are a reliable friend!
- *I respect your insight and your judgment.* I have you marked as very wise, insightful, and intelligent. I'll welcome your evaluation, diagnosis, and appraisal of who I am and where I am. And I believe you can help me assess what direction my life should take.
- *I believe in you.* You treat me like I'm a

good person. That makes you a good person. You must be, for it takes one to know one!

- *I'm listening to you.* I'm going to be completely honest. For the first time in my life, I am living in a world I've never lived in before. Call it humility. Tell me which of my answers is wrong. I've always been so sure I knew it all. When I have been criticized, I always assumed that my critics were wrong and I was right.

  Be honest with me, even if you know I won't like what you tell me! Believe me, I've changed! I don't want my way and my will. I just don't want to continue making mistakes like I have been!

  I'm not Jesus. I'm a human being, and that means I'm not perfect. I'm not ego-oriented; I'm success-oriented! I don't listen for compliments; I'm looking and listening for wisdom! I don't want my own way. I just want to find the right way."

Now that you're open to help, find a special small group of persons who can relate to who, what, and where you are. They'll help you on the humility and honesty path.

THE POWER OF SMALL GROUPS

For an alcoholic, there's AA (Alcoholics Anonymous). I cannot recommend this organization too highly when alcohol or drugs are part of the problem.

Small groups that understand and care about your hurt—however horrific—are meeting quietly, prayerfully near you. Seek out a positive house of faith, and you'll find one.

In the Crystal Cathedral, we have over twenty small groups that welcome and help fellow human beings who have been going through pain. We founded the first Suiciders Anonymous group at the Crystal Cathedral over thirty years ago. We have three small groups that are made up only of persons who are victims of incest abuse.

Pray for help and guidance, and God will connect you with a person and a place where you can honestly and humbly let it all hang out. This person will laugh with you and be honest enough to tell you what you must hear. And he or she won't reject you if you don't do what the group wisely advises.

The people in small groups know they're dealing with a hurting heart that still has a way to go before it can accept help from those who are really trying to rescue, release, and renew a friend.

They love you! You've got to believe that. God lives, and He loves you. He's reaching out to you, using these faces, eyes, tongues, and touches. Let God give your pained self a holy hug through the hearts and with the arms of those who are close to you.

If the small group you choose is AA or another small group for persons with chemical addictions, be ready to stay with that small-group therapy as long as you live. But when you find and feel the recovery, be prepared to stop using this clique as your warm blanket. Start your own small group. Reach into your world and be available to replicate this healing therapy.

Next, find your one essential friend (O.E.F.) and make this relationship the highest priority on your list of friends, relatives, and acquaintances.

ONE ESSENTIAL FRIEND

Your one essential friend is the one person where ego and fear of rejection play no part whatsoever.

For me that one essential friend became

my wife before she became my O.E.F. Arvella and I were married in 1950. We're approaching our fiftieth wedding anniversary. God alone knows how Arvella has helped me turn my hurts into halos. How swift she is to see the direction of my reaction to negative experiences. How strongly and skillfully she'll admonish, advise, and correct me if I'm not handling an issue wisely and well. And when she advises me to talk to one person or another, I'll do it with a listening mind and a humble, receptive heart!

I cannot tell you where to find your O.E.F.

But try a positive-thinking house of faith, because you will need an O.E.F. who shares your growing spiritual self. Now you will embrace a new, refreshing relationship with the God revealed in the Holy Bible.

Look for a positive-thinking church where there are Bible classes. Check it out. If they're positive, stay there. If they are negative, dogmatic, nonhumble, and critical of other churches and houses of worship—check out. You can do better.

Stop and settle down when and where you can feel the spiritual vibrations of a God of love. Stop and stay if Jesus Christ—the greatest religious thinker and leader of all time—is honored, respected, and listened to respectfully.

You can't find a more helpful faith than Christianity. Jesus knew God better than any other religious teacher. Many of us believe *He came to make God real to me*.

He's my Savior. He is my Ultimate and Eternal O.E.F.! In His spirit and presence I learn to be humble and honest.

7
There's a Halo Hidden in Every Hurt

You're ready to say "hello" to a halo!

Don't miss the halos that are all around you. I call them "hurting hearts halo crowned."

The unquenchable human spirit can be found in every age, race, culture, and academic level! What beautiful proof of the presence of that Eternal Creative Holy Spirit we call God!

Yes, we all see what we look for. The negative-thinking person sees only suffering, sadness, and sickness, while the possibility thinker sees *hurting hearts halo crowned!*

But don't look for sinless saints. They're not to be found.

And don't look for holy hearts who never make any of those common mistakes that mark humans. Such folk don't exist.

Where do you look to find holy hearts? In monasteries? In churches? In hallowed halls of holy worship? Could be!

In hospitals? Among the nurses and doctors? Yes. But take special note of the patients, even those asleep in a coma. They're still alive. They haven't chosen suicide. They'll bravely battle this day's challenge and not give up, no matter how devastating the hurt.

If you want to identify hurting hearts halo crowned, look for six characteristics.

First, look for people who achieve in spite of extreme adversity.

1. People Who Achieve Over Extreme Adversity

After I made a mission to the Orient, I returned to Hawaii to finish my book. Guess what?

I received a fax in my room. My dear, dear friend, Senator Max Cleland, had called my California office to speak to me and had been told, "He's not in. He's in Hawaii."

He was shocked. "That's where I am!" he said.

So we connected. It had been a couple of years since we were together. Max extended his only arm with a loud laugh. "Congratulations, Bob! The last time I saw you, you were sitting in the front row of the gallery for the President's State of the Union address!"

"Thanks, Max. I saw you sitting in your wheelchair down among the senators, and I waved at you! I'm so proud of you! Congratulations, Senator Max Cleland!"

As the hours wore on, I asked him what I had never—in our twenty-year friendship—dared ask before. "Max, you had both legs and your right arm blown off in Vietnam. How come you didn't bleed to death? My daughter, Carol, lost only one leg in her accident and took seventeen and a half pints of blood!"

"I took forty pints, Bob! The only reason I didn't bleed to death in five minutes was that the shrapnel hit so close to the flames it partially seared the severed ends of the blood vessels in my arm and legs."

"Tell me, Max, what was the worst part of that hellish experience?" I asked.

"When I got home, Bob, for a year and a half I was devastated. I could only sit with my body, which had no legs, no thighs, and I could do nothing. I had no job. I had only one arm and one hand. Day after day, month after month, it was simply devastating—that's the only word I can use. Here I was, twenty-eight years old, and I had no future. I was a hero. So I had only one thing—a recognized name in my town in Georgia. Then I got a wild idea. I'd run for a political office. I did and was elected to the state senate.

"Sure, I turned my scar into a star! I'll admit it. Then, when my governor, Jimmy Carter, was elected president, he appointed me head of the Veterans Affairs in Washington. And when Senator Sam Nunn retired, I ran for office, got elected, and here I am! I have my own seat in the United States Senate, and it still gives me a thrill. My name is on my senate seat!

"Yes, Bob. I wouldn't be where I am without these scars. It's a heck of a way to get there! But here I am and enjoying every minute of it!"

I looked at him and saw it—a halo. Yes, the radiance rises from the aura of achievement over extreme adversity!

Three weeks later, Max was at the Crystal Cathedral to receive one of my Scars into Stars awards. After the ceremony, a petite, black-haired woman timidly approached the stage. "May I meet Mr. Cleland, please?" she begged the staff.

Max saw the encounter and reached out

his only good hand. She cried, sobbing, "I had to meet you. I am from Vietnam. I am so sorry for what my country did to you."

"Don't worry," Max assured her. "I love you!"

"Oh, thank you!" she responded through her tears.

Wow! That's a halo. Yes, God is proud of Max Cleland. He's a hurting heart, halo-crowned.

Look around you. A child in braces. An old man with two canes. A teenager in a wheelchair. They demonstrate an unconquerable human spirit. Their spirit is awesome. Say hello to their halo!

If you want to see other hurting hearts that have been halo crowned, look for people who will not give up their faith.

2. People Who Will Not Give Up Their Faith

J. Wallace Hamilton tells of his sister Jan, who with her husband, Reg, went as a missionary to Kenya, Africa. They had a nine-year-old son. A brilliant, happy boy, he was sent to a special boarding school for missionary children, three hundred miles from the primitive area where his mother and father worked.

One day the child suddenly contracted pneumonia and died before his parents could reach him. School children gathered carnations and roses from all the gardens. The natives made a cedar casket, and the boy was buried under the green grass.

In his mother's first letter home to her pastor brother, J. Wallace Hamilton, her first sentence was, "The Lord has trusted us with a great sorrow." She was a living example of a sentence in the Bible, "We triumph even in our troubles" (Romans 5:3, Moffatt translation).

Check the heroes around you! They achieve over extreme adversity, they will not give up their faith, and they refuse to give up on their dreams, even though the road is harder than anyone can imagine.

3. People Who Refuse to Give Up on Their Dream

When my son was a freshman in college, he had a tough time with a course in Russian. He said, "Dad, I think I'm going to quit it." He didn't. Perhaps I helped him with what I did.

I was in New York and saw this huge poster of a football player. He was sitting on the bench, he'd thrown down his helmet, mud was on his face, tears were rolling from his eyes, and his elbows were on his knees. He was dejected. The big words underneath read: *I quit.*

In a bottom corner of the poster, shown from far away, was a picture of a black hill, and on the hill was a cross. Underneath the cross were the words: *I didn't.*

I bought the poster and gave it to my son.

Connect with a winner. His name is Jesus Christ.

Then you will catch a fresh image of who you are. You are a special child of God. As a follower of Jesus Christ, you give up the option of giving up.

If you want to see other hearts halo crowned, also look for persons who achieve the impossible, never letting their disabilities limit their awesome achievements.

4. People Who Achieve the Impossible

Not long ago, I watched in awe a story on the CBS program *Sixty Minutes*. Unfolding before me was a most intriguing interview with a dynamic, beautiful young woman. Now, I have met and interviewed some of the most phenomenal people who have overcome incredible odds to turn their hurts into halos. Yet I was struck by the tenacity of this young woman.

Evelyn Glennie was born and bred in Scotland, where she was raised on a farm. Evelyn had a profound interest in music. She excelled in playing percussion instruments, so much that in 1982 she was accepted as a student in London's Royal Academy of Music. That's no small feat for any musician. But Evelyn is profoundly deaf.

Although she was born into a hearing world, the nerves in her ears started to deteriorate when she was six. By the time she was eleven, Evelyn was so hard of hearing that she was given hearing aids. But according to Evelyn, losing her hearing was not going to end her love of music.

"There was no way I was going to change my life because of this one little statement," she told Ed Bradley in the television profile.

One little statement? Deafness is a little statement? Wow! I knew then and there that Evelyn is an exceptional person. For most people, losing something as fundamental as hearing is a hurt that might completely crush them. But to look at deafness as "one little statement" unveils the inner strength and courage of a remarkable human being who has her priorities squared away!

Evelyn threw away her hearing aids because, "In a musical sense, they boosted the sound, and that meant the clarity was lost." Instead she used her other senses to help "hear" the music.

Her intuition and persistence paid off. Soon, not only was Evelyn performing in some of the greatest concert halls in the world, but the greatest orchestras were there to accompany her. Evelyn has been center stage in some of the greatest concert halls, giving performances that stun and delight the hardest critics.

The greatest mystery is how she knows when to come in on cue. With the first strike of her kettledrum, she commands the stage with power and grace. Yet she never hears the music that backs her up. She has to lip-read the conductor, which is complicated by the fact that his face is not always in view as he directs the entire orchestra. Yet Evelyn never seems to miss a beat.

From xylophone to marimba to piano to drums, Evelyn's concerts feature her on more than a dozen instruments. Her husband, a sound engineer, helps coordinate her extensive travel needs, including the tracking of all her instruments. She now has the luxury of selecting which composer will write a concerto especially for her.

Ms. Glennie's enthusiasm bubbled over in her *Sixty Minutes* interview. Watching her, you quickly forgot that she is deaf. She lip-read Ed Bradley's questions perfectly and even suggested that he had an American accent! She could detect it, she said, by the way he moved his lips. Her love for life leaped out of the television screen, and I wished I could attend just one of her concerts, for I know it would be one of the most moving and emotional musical performances ever.

Yet as I watched this dynamic person, I was struck by how easy it would have been for her to have taken a different path in life—one of bitterness, anger, or resentment that life cheated her out of such a rich entitlement as sound.

What a loss the world would now know if Evelyn had let her hurt enwrap her and entangle her into giving up the one thing she truly excelled at—music.

Evelyn cannot hear the music she creates. She cannot enjoy the sound of her instruments. She cannot be rewarded audibly with applause at the end of a performance. Surely, this young lady would give anything to change that—to be able to hear the symphony of her works.

> *"There is in every heart a spark of heavenly fire which lies dormant in the broad daylight of prosperity, but which kindles up and beams and blazes in the dark hour of adversity."*
>
> —WASHINGTON IRVING
> ESSAYIST, NOVELIST, AND HISTORIAN (1783–1859)

Ed Bradley asked her, "If there were a miracle and your hearing were to be restored, what would your reaction be?"

I should have guessed the answer. Her life has lived it to date. But no. I was shocked.

"I think you know," she said, "I have already the miracle of being able to play music . . . to find that aspect in life that pleases me. So that is my miracle. I can't ask for any more. I don't want any more."

Check the heroes around you! They achieve over adversity; they will not give up their faith; they refuse to give up on their dreams; they achieve the impossible; and they pick up the dream of a martyr.

5. Survivors Who Pick Up the Dream of a Martyr

Linda Biehl is such a mother.

Linda Biehl said goodbye to her daughter, Amy, in October 1992 for what was to have been a ten-month visit to South Africa to help support the antiapartheid movement.

Amy had been the captain of Stanford's diving team, which won the NCAA championship. She had studied international relations there and had started working in South African political affairs in Washington upon her graduation in 1989. In 1992 this twenty-six-year-old woman received a Fulbright Grant to study women and children in the emerging democracy.

As Amy readied to board the airplane in Los Angeles, she had reassured her tearful mother, "Don't cry, Mom."

Linda remembered those words during the months Amy was so far away in a strife-torn country. Then two days before Amy was to return home—to be reunited with her mom and dad and to attend Rutgers University to pursue her Ph.D.—she was tragically in the wrong place at the wrong time.

The blonde-haired athlete and scholar was driving a few South African friends back to a black township. She drove straight into a frenzied mob coming from a political rally where the slogan was "One settler, one bullet." The rally had whipped the crowd into a crazed state, which convinced them to kill the next white person they saw.

Amy was the only white person in that car. She never had a chance. Ironically, the very people she had come to help now brutally stoned and stabbed her to death.

News of her daughter's murder shattered Linda Biehl's serene life. Yet Linda's immediate thoughts were to recall Jesus' words that she had taught in her Sunday school Christian ethics class, "Father, forgive them, for they know not what they do."

Linda and her husband, Peter, now found themselves thrust into the center of a political turmoil. The four South Africans who killed their daughter were tried and convicted, but the Biehls understood that the door was not yet closed. Amy had told her parents about the Truth and Reconciliation Commission, a prenegotiated condition in

South Africa's new democracy that granted amnesty and forgiveness for politically directed crimes. It was inevitable that Amy's killers would soon apply for amnesty themselves.

In May 1997, South African officials notified the Biehls that Amy's killers had indeed applied for amnesty. Bishop Desmond Tutu, who headed the Truth and Reconciliation Commission, spoke to the Biehls at length about the process. He told them, "You must speak what's in your heart at the hearing."

Linda and Peter Biehl knew their daughter's convictions. Amy had done a lot of work on the declaration of human rights with Dela Omar, who is now the minister of justice in South Africa. The Biehls felt that 80 percent of the people in South Africa had been controlled by 20 percent of the country. The Biehls knew it was right to forgive the four young men, and they encouraged them to live a good life.

"We realized the process was important to South Africa," Linda explained, "and we knew Amy understood their oppression. We knew why those young men killed Amy. When we were in South Africa for the hearing, we went to the squatter camps and townships outside Cape Town and saw the conditions they lived in. Had I been a young person in South Africa, I would have had a lot to deal with too.

"At the hearing the four young men actually confessed to Amy's murder and asked us for forgiveness. We were at peace with ourselves because we were able to forgive them." (The men were released in the summer of 1998 after serving four and one-half years in prison.)

The Biehls not only forgave their daughter's murderers, but they also established a foundation in her name to carry on her work. The Amy Biehl Foundation provides South African youth with educational scholarships and social programs, giving them the opportunities they need to succeed. In a lot of South African communities, 80 to 90 percent of the people are unemployed and do not have the education to get a job. The Foundation works to help Africans develop skills like welding, sewing, and block making.

In March 1998 the Biehls learned that Victor, the ambulance driver who had attended Amy, was undergoing counseling because he had seen so much violence and ugliness through his seventeen years of driving an ambulance. When Amy was killed, it apparently shattered him.

The driver's therapist asked the Biehls to talk to him. At a dinner together they mentioned, "Victor, there is no first aid out in the township schools."

Victor was excited by the prospect of doing something about that. "I can do that," he said.

Since that meeting, the Biehls and Victor have trained more than three hundred people in the area outside Cape Town in first aid, including South African police officers who had no training and teachers in schools that today are completely equipped with first-aid kits.

"I feel liberated and energized," Linda concluded. "I have been blessed with the ability to understand much more about the world. You don't always know that until you come to the wall. Amy talked a lot about breaking her pain threshold when she was a swimmer. Once you do it, you want to do it again and again."

After Amy's death, one of Amy's professors at Stanford wrote the Biehls and said,

"Once in a while you have a student who goes out and does what you teach."

Linda's wish is that Jesus Christ would think of her in the same way. "I wish He would think of me as being one of His students doing His will," she says.

These words from a grieving mother, one whose heart has been halo crowned.

If you want to see other hearts halo crowned, look for persons God is proud of!

6. Persons God Is Proud Of

The spiritual aura that you sense surrounding some special soul marks the presence of a heavenly Father who is proud of how one of His children is turning a hurt into a halo and a scar into a star. The Bible keeps referring to God as our heavenly Father. He is surely capable of the holy pride of a father who is proud of the achievements of one of His children.

I'm sure the heavenly Father is proud of William and Kay Keck and their daughter Anne.

The morning of September 12 was just another school day. William normally got the kids up while his wife showered. This morning turned out to be different.

As William awakened Anne, he realized she was curled up in a fetal position with a glazed stare on her face. She was rigid. He could not make her stir.

William yelled for his wife, and she came running. Kay immediately recognized Anne's condition as a seizure.

The next twelve hours were a whirlwind. By dark the Kecks knew a little bit more. The doctor's words that evening will never leave their minds: "We think we know what is wrong with Anne. She has tuberous sclerosis, a genetic disorder that causes benign tumors in many major organs. All you can do is take her home and give her lots of love."

When William and Kay first found out this devastating news, they didn't know what to do. Would Anne live or die? The doctor did not really say.

Anger entered their lives. "God, how could you do this to us? What did we do wrong as parents? Whose side of the family did this genetic defect come from?" Their minds worked overtime as September 12 moved to 13, 14, 15, and on.

During the subsequent weeks the Kecks' prayers seemed to go unanswered. Kay and William cried and prayed a lot in private. What was ahead of them? The fear of the unknown seemed overwhelming.

Yet each day seemed a little better. They started to search medical books and magazines to find information about this disorder. They solicited second opinions from other doctors. Yes, Anne had tuberous sclerosis (TS). They could not escape the fact.

Soon they realized they had two options. They could let TS ruin their lives, probably destroying their family and their marriage, or they could take the hand they were dealt and move forward. As Kay and William held each other in pain, they made a commitment to each other and God: to move on.

The rest of this story is told in a chronology of events.

- Early kindergarten year: Doctors said that Anne might never be able to write.
- End of first grade: Anne received the penmanship award.
- Middle of first grade: Doctors said that Anne would probably have to read using

the sight-word method. Phonetics didn't seem to make sense to her.

- End of fifth grade: Anne's teachers said she reads better phonetically than 95 percent of her regular classmates. (No, Anne is not on grade level in reading, but she has made great strides.)

By the time Anne was in third grade, the Kecks were trying to be more open with others about TS and Anne's challenges. They wrote her story and gave a copy to each third grader. Anne's teacher encouraged the children and their parents to talk about Anne and her disease. Soon Anne's acceptance among her schoolmates increased. She began to receive birthday and slumber party invitations.

At present Anne is in the seventh grade. She is a cheerleader, a gymnast, and an active member of the "middler" group of the Kecks' church, where she sings in the choir.

She wakes up in the morning with a smile on her face. God is proud of Anne Keck and her parents, William and Kay.

God is proud of you when you keep the faith and do not allow anger or bitterness to come in. God is also proud of how beautifully you handle your hardship. Neighbors, friends, and even people you don't know are saying beautiful things about your great attitude and your beautiful spirit.

You can't see it in the mirror, but you are wearing a halo, for you are sharing courage and hope with all who watch you! That hallowed spirit around you is the presence of God, your heavenly Father. God's pride is showing! Your personality is the reflection of the beauty of Christ's spirit within you! Hallelujah!

Yes, the halo is found in the triumph of human dignity over adversity. The human spirit can radiate through hardship.

I recently reread one of my favorite books, *What About Tomorrow?* by J. Wallace Hamilton. He was one of the greatest Christian authors of his time. He had a remarkable insight into how hurts can become halos.

I was touched by his words, and chose to include a couple of pages from his wonderful book. Here's what he says:

I like to think that God, too, is often proud of His sons, as we are proud of our sons when they take the step and climb the hill, carry their sorrows bravely, and stand up against the storm and have dominion.

Don't you believe God was proud of Job that day when everything was swept away, when he lifted his boil-covered arm to heaven, and said, "Though he slay me, yet will I trust in him"?

I tell you, this dignity of man in defeat, the resiliency of the human spirit that rises unbroken above adversity, is part of the gladness of God in the glory of His creation. And of course that is what the cross means, at least in part, and why it holds our hearts in a holy hush, far more an emblem of triumph than of tragedy—a Man walking up the hill, taking the step, taking the hammer blows, and turning them into blessings.

Maybe you will have to do that too, climb the hill with that cross of yours, whatever it is—with no miracle to make it easy.

A woman going through trouble said, "I wish I had never been made."

And a friend said to her, "My dear, you're not made yet, you're just being made."

That is good theology. Man is not made yet, he is just being made. He is being made by his struggle with the imperfect and unfinished, he is being made by the big dream in him that lifts him though he may not reach it; and he is being made by the hammer blows of life, the hardships he endures and the crosses he carries. Strong hands are on your life and they are the hands, as Jesus said, of a Father."

Check the heroes around you!
They achieve over adversity.
They will not give up their faith.
They refuse to give up on their dreams.
They achieve the impossible.
They pick up the dream of a martyr.

They are people God is proud of, and they are persons who have experienced a miracle.

7. Persons Who Have Experienced a Miracle

Phil Gilbert successfully worked hard for his many achievements. It was a formula learned from his father: When faced with a problem, work at it. This was the approach he believed would overcome his latest difficulty—infertility.

Phil and his wife, Marilyn, sought out the

"I'd rather be in this wheelchair with God than on my feet without Him. In heaven I look forward to folding up my wheelchair, handing it to Jesus, and saying straight from the heart, 'Thanks, I needed that.' "

—JONI EARECKSON TADA

AUTHOR AND DISABILITY ADVOCATE

best infertility clinic in the nation. The doctors narrowed the problem down to Phil and quickly scheduled a battery of tests and treatments. Confident that the medical institution would resolve the issue, Phil faithfully followed all of the doctor's orders and treatments.

Three years later, however, the situation remained the same. Phil and his wife could not conceive. Having exhausted all medical possibilities, the doctors called Phil in for a consultation. "There is nothing more we can try," they reported. "We know of no other treatments. We're sorry."

Phil left the doctors' office feeling dejected and depressed. For the first time in his life, no matter how hard he worked to overcome his problem, there was no solution. It was a hurt he had never before experienced. How would he tell his wife? How could they overcome their shattered dreams? How would they go on without the possibility of having their own family?

The next morning as he was getting ready to go to work, Phil hopped in the shower. As the warm water washed over him, tears streamed down his face; he felt the deepest pain he had ever known.

Alone and despondent, Phil turned his thoughts toward God. He had never felt much need for God in his life before. His self-sufficient attitude had left little room for a personally involved Creator. But now, perhaps, God was his only hope. As the warm water mingled tears with soothing spray, Phil called out to God.

"Suddenly," Phil recalled, "I heard a voice within me say, *Get on your knees*. It wasn't so much an audible voice, but an internal one that could not be debated.

" 'I'm not getting on my knees in the shower,' I argued. But again, I felt the urge. *Get on your knees*. Again, I hesitated, but again, I was compelled. *Get on your knees*. The message was clear, and so I did.

"Time stood still as I cried on the floor of that shower. I don't know how long I was kneeling, praying, and crying, but when I finally did get up, the water was cold. I had experienced the peace of God for the very first time. I also knew immediately that I was healed."

Phil waited anxiously for his wife to come home. When she did, she was dejected. "I thought maybe I was pregnant," she confessed. "My period was late, so I went to the doctor hoping . . . but I'm not."

As Phil consoled Marilyn, he held her face gently and said, "I'm not sure I know how to explain this, but I *know* you will be. I'm healed . . ." and he revealed the entire story.

Three months later, Phil was an expectant father! He returned to the infertility clinic to happily confront his doctor and report the good news. Four children later, Phil and Marilyn still give God complete credit for the miracle of their family.

The halo surrounding the Gilbert family shines brightly, reminding them all that God does perform miracles.

Miracles! They're all around you. "A hundred million miracles are happening every day," the musical line goes. In this world so afflicted with sin, suffering, evil, and injustice, how is it possible that there are still so many emotionally healthy humans?

Quite simple—the miracles keep on coming! New weddings. New conceptions. New babies are being born. Look for joyously happy people, and you'll feel a radiance and a presence. The happy presence is God, who's there to accept our thanksgiving.

Don't miss the halos that are all around you!

8
Never Give Up Hope!

Charles Beard was one of our great American historians. When he came to the end of his career, he was asked what great lessons he had learned from history. He answered, "I've learned four. First: Whom the gods would destroy, they first made mad with power. Second: I've learned the mills of God grind slowly, yet they grind exceedingly fine. Third: I've learned the bee fertilizes the flower it robs. Fourth: I've learned that when it's dark enough, you'll be able to see the stars."

So become a *hope-a-holic*. I am living with an incurable hope addiction. Whatever happens, I have an incurable, instinctive, impulsive, impertinent tendency to sense and to surrender to a feeling of hope, because I know tomorrow is coming. I know yesterday is a cancelled check. Today is cash in my hand, to spend as I want. Tomorrow is a promissory note from God Almighty. That's where I live. That makes me an incurable hope-a-holic. And the hope that I talk about, I promise you, will not disappoint you. All of your hope may not be fulfilled, but hope will fill your today with the emotional gift of optimism. So hope is its own immediate reward.

Never, Never, Never Give Up on Hope, No Matter What Anyone Says!

Hope has long had its detractors. Possibility-thinking medical doctors have often been criticized for building "false hope." Years ago, a well-known physician, Dr. Bernie Siegel, handled that criticism brilliantly with this awesome insight: "The only false hope is no hope."

We must go all the way back to Greek philosophy to see the hit that hope had to take.

In Greek mythology, Zeus became very angry with the way human beings behaved and betrayed each other, so he decided to punish the human race. He found an agent by the name of Pandora and gave her a box which held all of the evils of the world. She could lift the lid, release the evils, and punish human beings as they deserved.

Well, you know the story. Pandora's box

was opened, and all the evils flew out except for one. An evil called *hope*. The Greeks, with all their philosophers—Socrates, Aristotle, Plato—basically looked on hope as an evil, for hope betrayed human beings. They reasoned: Ultimately we're all going to die. So all hope is ultimately false hope.

So the plays in Greek tradition were never happy-ending stories. They always ended with a bad scene. That's why they're called Greek tragedies.

The greatest Greek tragedy, however, was that even with their advanced philosophies, neither Aristotle, Socrates, Plato, nor anyone else in that great culture discovered that hope is not an evil but instead is the most positive virtue.

Along came the apostle Paul, who was very well educated. He debated Greek friends, claiming hope as one of the three crowning holy virtues of life: Faith, hope, and love. Imagine how shocking and revolutionary that thinking was.

Where did Paul get it? He was a scholarly Jew. He knew his Old Testament. And the theme of the Old Testament, in a word, is *hope*.

Hope did not come into human thinking through philosophy, psychology, or any scientific discovery. It has its roots in the Old Testament. It is a gift that God shared with the Jewish people. Jesus Christ was educated and imbued with this faith, and He embraced hope! So the New Testament is the ultimate book of hope.

In 1959, one of this century's leading psychiatrists, Dr. Karl Menninger, delivered a major address of global significance at the 115th annual meeting of the American Psychiatry Association in Philadelphia, Pennsylvania. I'm so proud that he sent an autographed copy of his lecture to me. Its title is one word: "Hope."

You can choose to be hopeful in your hurt. For never before in history has there been a day like tomorrow.

Eight years later, in 1967, I found myself in Madrid, Spain, with four thousand psychiatrists from around the world at the Fourth International Meeting of Psychiatrists. Here I heard a lecture on hope, given by the German psychiatrist H. W. Janz. I received from the Library of Congress a copy of that entire address, entitled "Hope in Psychotherapy, 1967, H.W. Janz, Madrid, Spain." On page 1 he says how little or nothing has been done by psychiatry on the subject of hope:

> "Psychology and psychiatry have pretty much walked away from this subject because it has religious overtones," he said. "The only really significant work done on hope was done by Karl Menninger in 1959."

With cynicism and secularism, spreading agnosticism and atheism, people want to believe that they can live hurt-free, fulfilled, happy lives without religion, without God, without hope. "Psychiatry is afraid of hope," I heard Dr. Janz say at that international meeting. "Because it leads people to think spiritually, and then they encounter what they think may be something religious."

But without hope where does that leave hurting humans? Dr. Janz answered that question, "Let me tell you about a forty-two-year-old patient of mine. She's single. She's female. And here is her life without hope. This is what she wrote:

> Nonfulfillment of love removed me from the world. Not only the world of

> man, but the interconnection of the whole world. It made me completely stiff. I am empty and burned out inside. I move like a puppet with stiff, jerky movements. A constant depression puts holes in my soul like a cancer. I am split. Broken apart in pieces. There are no impulses anymore. Spontaneity is no longer possible. Music hurts.

In the last half of this century, psychiatry is beginning to embrace hope as a healing, positive force. For psychiatry to make such a move is significant, for Sigmund Freud did not support "religion." Some scholars suggest that the rise of this young science called psychiatry in the twentieth century was an effort to invent an emotional support system for atheists. For millenniums the positive religion from the Holy Bible inspired a positive faith that satisfied the deep emotional needs of anguishing humans. So it is easy to see how the inventors and developers of an emotional support system for nonreligious persons would be inclined to reject hope.

Then Dr. Karl Menninger led his profession into this revolutionary respect for hope. He did it using the empirical test procedures of science. In his classic lecture on hope, he tells about experiments where they gave placebos in testing new drugs. He wrote, "The shocking thing was not that the people who got the new drugs definitely had a marked improvement that proved that the drug was good.

"But," he said, "again and again, the people that got the placebos had the same shocking healing record." Why did they suddenly begin to recover? The placebo effect gave them hope! "The mystery healing force of hope was scientifically affirmed," Dr. Menninger claimed in his historic address.

I remember a member of my church who became very ill. Due to her extreme mental illness, she was confined to a locked room. I visited her there many times. I don't recall how many months she was there without any change for the better or worse.

Suddenly one day when I visited, she was a totally different person. She was perfectly normal and back to her youthful spirit. I said, "Mary*, what happened?!"

"Oh," she said, "you know I have been sick. I realize now how sick I was. You know why I was sick, Dr. Schuller? I felt I was in hell!

---

*Name has been changed.

About ten days ago," she said, "I got a new doctor." She continued, "He came and said to me, 'Mary, I'm your new doctor. My name is Dr. Heaven.'

"And I said, 'What?'

"He said, 'My name is Dr. Heaven.'

"I couldn't believe it. I said, 'You can't be here. This is hell! How can heaven be in hell?'

"He said, 'I'm Dr. Heaven. You're with me now.' "

She said, "I kept saying, well, it's not hell anymore because heaven is here."

Totally illogical, yes. But Mary kept repeating that thought to herself! She suddenly believed she was not in hell, but in heaven. That was enough to change her thinking and allow hope to come in with its healing, life-changing, empowering spirit. Her skin changed color, and her eyes were no longer dull or drugged; they sparkled with life and energy.

That hope was the very presence of a new spirit that carried the name *God*. Her healing happened and held for thirty-three years. She just passed away as I wrote this book!

Hope often is the very presence and the power of God within you.

To find the healing power of hope, we return to its spiritual source—religious faith. Positive religion tackles and wins the final argument of death. With hope, death is not a tragedy; it is a happy ending. We have lived our lives; we have borne fruit. The flower has blossomed. The petals fall. We have finished the course with arrival power, survival power, and now revival power. We know where we're going, and hope will not disappoint us!

You find this hope in the faith found in the Bible. You find it in Jesus Christ. He will never disappoint you. Become a friend of Jesus. Become a friend of the Bible. You will find a faith that will keep hope alive forever.

How I Became a Hope-a-holic

Here's my personal testimony. I don't have a strong testimony of someone who "was into drugs, alcohol, and sexual sins . . . then I found Jesus and I was converted, born again, and have given up all those sins." No, my testimony is quite different.

My father and mother were God-fearing people. They read the Bible every day in the home. They took their children to church every single Sunday morning. They prayed for us, and we had our prayers with them, around the breakfast table, the noontime table, the evening table, and at the bed. They played the piano in our home and we sang hymns. As a child sitting on the piano bench with my mother, I learned to sing "Jesus loves me, this I know, for the Bible tells me so. Little ones to Him belong, they are weak, but He is strong."[1]

So that's where my faith is coming from. That's why I can testify to this Bible verse, "You are my hope, O Lord God; You are my trust from my youth" (Psalm 71:5).

I had a happy childhood because it was filled with hopes. And the hopes gave birth to beautiful dreams.

YOU NEED HOPE when . . .

- you get a dream. Whether you are a child, a young person, or an older person, hope lifts that dream until drive and energy come into your personality, and you go for it and take a chance. You need hope when you're dreaming of your future.

YOU NEED HOPE when . . .

- these dreams run into despairing problems, obstacles, difficulties, and frustrations. You need hope to protect you from the assault of anger, fear, worry, or anxiety. You need hope when you're moving your dreaming into actions.

YOU NEED HOPE when . . .

- you're healthy. And you need it when you're in ill health.

YOU NEED HOPE when . . .

- you apply for college and after you're in the university. Then when you choose a career, you will need hope to lift you and lead you onward and upward and forward.

YOU NEED HOPE when . . .

- you're young and are looking for a girlfriend or boyfriend. And then, when you fall in love, you need it to propose marriage. When you get married, you need hope as much as, if not more than, ever. Hope is what you need when the baby comes and you hold that infant in your arms.

YOU NEED HOPE when . . .

- you're dying. And you need hope in all of your living.

There will be no love without it. Hope is what will keep your faith alive. That's why hope is right in the middle of the holy trinity of human emotions, "faith, hope, and love."

What Is This Thing Called Hope?

Hope. It is a marvelous, mysterious mood that comes into your personality. Suddenly your load is lifted, color returns to your skin, and your eyes get their sparkle back. What is it? It is a scientific experience of the presence of God operating in your personality.

Are you an agnostic or an atheist? You say you don't believe in God? Wait a minute. God believes in you. You have had times when you were in despair and you got through it. Somebody or something came and encouraged you. Or you got a bright idea. Or things changed. Or you got lucky. Again and again your good luck was really your good Lord.

You may not believe in Him, but God believes in you, even if you are an atheist. He is not going to cast you out without offering you hope. Hope is a mystery. When it happens in the personality, it can only be scientifically described as the presence of a God of love coming into your mind, your spirit, your body, your personality! This is God. This is hope!

Our ministry of one-half century has focused on hope. Hope. Hope. At the end of every Crystal Cathedral service, you are going to feel better. Critics would say, "Oh, it's a feel-good kind of a religion." You bet it is. If we bring God into your life, you're not going to feel bad. We are a gospel-preaching church, and *gospel* means "good news."

And if we give you good news, you'll really feel hopeful.

Find the Faith That Makes You a Hope-a-holic

How can you find this kind of faith? Try adopting these five goals.

1. *Find a faith that inspires a healthy optimism.*

You can choose to be hopeful in your hurt, for never before in history has there been a day like tomorrow. Tomorrow has never before happened.

> *Look!*
> *Tomorrow is on*
> *stage . . .*
> *Watch the curtain rise!*
> *Get ready for*
> *a happy surprise!*

And tomorrow will be different than today or yesterday. Yes, yesterday is gone. Tomorrow is coming on. And tomorrow is a gift! We pay no fee for each new day. The sunrise is free!

Tomorrow may even be better than you can imagine. Yes, today is pregnant with tomorrow! Tomorrow is inevitable—nothing can delay its arrival. And tomorrow is only a few hours away.

The only thing between today and tomorrow is tonight. And that's when the stars come out!

So never give up on hope! Don't drop the curtain on tomorrow.

2. Choose a faith that focuses on personhood.

Faith should make you aware that you were designed and created to be a person, not just part of a crowd of people. Our ministry tries to turn people into persons. There is quite a difference between people and persons. A person is somebody who is aware that he or she makes decisions that the community cannot make for him or her. Deciding to have faith is a private, personal matter. Faith helps you mature and motivates you to think for yourself.

I just came back from visiting China, where I was the first person approved by China to lead a seminar in a hotel open to the public!

But getting official approval wasn't easy. I had to submit in writing what I was going to talk about. It went through a variety of levels and almost got torpedoed because the government had a problem when they heard I was telling people to "think."

"We don't want people to think," the Chinese officials said. "We want them to learn. We want them to listen. We want them to obey. But if people are motivated to think for themselves, we're going to have anarchy. We've got a billion people here!"

Hope-building faith comes from the Old and New Testaments. Here's a faith that declares that every individual soul was designed by God to be a distinctive person. You are to do your own thinking. You are to make up your own mind. That's the heart of real Christianity! All of this means a "true person" becomes a thoughtful manager of ideas.

3. Choose a faith that motivates you to manage ideas.

There is a large assortment of leadership management that's distributed around the world today, but our Crystal Cathedral ministry has something distinctive to lay on the table. You can go to universities and study

Yesterday is where it was . . .
Today is where it is . . .
Tomorrow is where
it's going to be.

Yes, tomorrow is coming!
Yesterday is tomorrow's grandparent.
Today is tomorrow's mother.
Tomorrow is the new child!
The next generation.

courses on how to manage money. Good. How to manage time. Good.

We focus on how to manage ideas. That's crucial. That's basic. But this is threatening to many secular minds. For when you train people to become idea managers, they may become possibility thinkers. They're being set up to be open to the proactive possibility of a good God investing in this cosmic universe! To nonreligious secularists, this business of turning people into thinking persons is pretty threatening.

To keep hope alive, you must learn how to manage the positive versus negative ideas that come into your head. Don't miss a great idea when it comes.

Next, you need to choose a faith that makes you proud of who you are.

4. Choose a faith that makes you proud of who you are.

Don't buy into the concept so many religions teach—that pride is always a sin. That's wrong.

I spent a few hours this week with Sir John Templeton, founder of the prestigious Templeton Fund and a dear friend. I said, "What are you doing these days?"

"Well," he said, "I'm preparing a new lecture on humility."

"Good," I responded. "Just realize that humility is not the opposite of pride."

He said, "What do you mean?"

"Well, the opposite of pride is not humility."

"Oh?" he said.

"No, the opposite of pride is shame. Humility and healthy pride are different sides of the same coin, heads and tails. And the coin has equal value, whether you've got heads up or tails up."

> *The opposite of pride is not humility. The opposite of pride is shame.*

The truly humble person is not ashamed of his humility; he feels good. He has healthy pride.

Healthy pride lets your faith give birth to strong self-respect. I'm proud of who I am. I'm proud of my wife. I'm proud of my kids. I'm proud of my church. I'm proud of my faith. I'm proud of my work."

"But," Sir John said, "the Bible says that pride is the beginning of the fall."

"Of course," I answered, "but, that word

pride is an English word, and it doesn't fully capture the deep dimensions of what I believe the Bible intends to teach. A better translation would be, *Egotism* always precedes the fall."

Egotism is demonic and very destructive. That's the difference. Dynamic faith will make you proud of who you are. Where will that lead you? To become a hope-a-holic!

Now you'll become a positive, possibility thinker. You'll never give up hoping no matter how old you are!

5. Choose a faith that you will never give up.

Some of my readers will remember Colonel Norman Vaughn. I have written about him in previous books. He is one of my heroes. Of all the people I've known and met, Colonel Norman Vaughn is tops. He accompanied Admiral Byrd on the Antarctic expedition in 1928, over seventy years ago. The last time I heard from him was when he—at the age of ninety—had climbed Mount Vaughn. That 10,000-foot mountain in the Antarctic was a mountain named after him by Admiral Byrd!

A recent letter from him told me what he's doing. He has a new dream. (He always does!)

"In the year 2005 I will be a hundred years old. And to celebrate my hundredth birthday, I'm planning to climb Mount Vaughn again. I have six of my guides preparing for it. They're already starting to save money so they can buy their tickets, but I hope to get some sponsors and that will help them. Now you ask me, Dr. Schuller, how can a hundred-year-old man climb a 10,302-foot mountain in Antarctica? Well, here's what I'm doing with my friends. When I start to wear out, I'm going to get on a plastic sled and let the six of them haul me to the top!"

What a powerful hope-a-holic!

This is what we are trying to do through our faith in God and in Jesus Christ and in the Holy Bible. And it all adds up to reality.

How can you become a hurt-healing hope-a-holic?

Practice possibility thinking and, while you are practicing it, you are living in the very presence of God! You move and He guides you, and nothing is impossible. He keeps your hope alive!

Many years ago a young man, Leland Stanford, Jr., died of typhoid fever just before his sixteenth birthday. After his death, his parents decided to found an institution in his memory. They visited several universities on the East Coast and discussed their ideas with the president of each university.

When they met with the president of Harvard, they asked how much a university would cost, in addition to land and buildings. The Harvard president told them, “I wouldn’t attempt that with an endowment smaller than five million dollars.” (This was in 1919.)

Leland’s parents were silent for a few moments, then Mr. Stanford said with a smile, “Well, Jane, we could manage that, couldn’t we?” And Mrs. Stanford nodded.

Mr. and Mrs. Stanford went back to California and founded Stanford University. The Stanfords turned their hurt into a halo and their scar into a star!

And you can too if you become a hope-a-holic. And to become a hope-a-holic, you must choose to have a living faith in God.

A Living Faith in God

“Okay, I’m beginning to be a believer in God, but how do I visualize Him?” you ask, adding, “I don’t know how to imagine Him.”

I’ll tell you how. Just picture in your mind

Jesus Christ. He came to this world to make God real, and He said, "He who has seen me has seen the Father." Do you want to see God in your mind and in your imagination? See Jesus Christ and follow Him!

I believe a positive idea is trying to get a hold in your mind. The idea calls for you to become a believer in the hope that not only can heal your hurt, but also can allow a new dream to emerge, which can turn into a new goal in your life. It's risky, of course! When God is leading you, you will always have to live and think and walk in His world—the world of faith.

God is constantly calling us to new horizons. God wants us to fly!

"Come to the edge," He said.

"It's dangerous there," I answered.

"Come to the edge," He said.

"It's risky. I might fall," I answered.

"Come to the edge. Trust me! Come to the edge," He said.

So I did. And He pushed me! And I flew!

9

The Hurting Heroes Hall of Fame

The inspiring stories of champions who transcend heartbreak have led me to conclude that every hurt can be a halo, every scar a star.

This chapter contains three of the most powerful true stories of people whom I admire for their ability to rise above their hurts. All three are close personal friends. Each one has been the recipient of my Scars into Stars award. They are lights in the darkness, shining to show that life goes on, even when you have experienced the worst of hurts.

I hope these stories are as inspiring to you as they are to me. The first people you'll meet in these pages are Steve and Mary Turville. Steve has been my personal photographer for many years, and his photography has been used on the jackets of my books. He has gathered my family for our annual Christmas picture, patiently waiting as grandchildren wiggled and teenagers complained. He photographed many of my children's weddings. He has been a dear friend.

His story, unfolding here, is one of tragic heartbreak. But it is filled with hope! Truly, he and his wife have turned their hurt into a halo.

Steve and Mary Turville

Steve and Mary Turville took a morning break from another busy day in their photography studio. Seeking relief in the air-conditioned restaurant nearby, the couple settled in for a quiet meal. Steve asked a blessing on their food, remembering to thank God for their family's health and well-being. It was a rich heritage, he thought, to realize that all of their children shared their love for God.

Steve's beeper abruptly ended the solitude. The studio was calling. Passing the bakery as he headed to the restaurant phone, Steve smelled the warm aroma and felt reassured. It was only when his studio manager answered that the sense of peace evaporated.

"Mr. Turville," the manager said breathlessly, "someone called from Colorado. He didn't make a lot of sense, but it sounded like something really bad happened. The man said it was urgent and left this number."

Steve and Mary's twenty-year-old son, Josh, had moved to the town of Bayfield, Colorado, just three months earlier from southern California. Working construction jobs on the side, Josh's real focus was to establish a youth ministry at the Bayfield Calvary Chapel. His love and support of young people included helping ex-convicts to become rehabilitated. Together with his two best friends, John Lara III and Steven Bates, the young men had stretched their hand out to one such eighteen-year-old, Joseph Gallegos, inviting him to be their fourth roommate.

Now Steve found himself calling the Colorado number, softly identifying himself, and trying to subdue the tide of fear welling up inside him.

Jeb Bryant, pastor of the Bayfield Calvary Church, broke the horrific news. "I went over to the house this morning after the police called me," he stammered. "There was a hostage situation with Joe," he said, crying and interrupting himself. "It's Josh, Steve, and John—they've all been murdered." Jeb's sobs echoed across the phone line.

Silence hung between the two men. As Steve's heart stopped, he heard himself asking, "Who? How? What are you saying?"

Jeb rambled on. "It looks like Joe went off his rocker and shot all three of the guys. He had been upset about his girlfriend breaking up with him. He just went crazy. After he killed the young men, Joe took Josh's 4 Runner and drove to the University of Northern Colorado in Greely to kill his girlfriend, who was attending college there. He took her and her roommates hostage for four hours before sharpshooters shot him."

Numbly, Steve hung up, his head swimming as he walked through a sea of people to find his wife still at the table. The phone call represented every parent's worst fear. Disbelief and denial swept over them as he spilled the news of their son's death. "Why?" was the question Mary asked no one in particular. "Joe had been doing so well. Why would he turn on them like that?"

The question was a puzzle that soon came together. Joe Gallegos, known as "Crazy Joe" to the local law enforcement authorities, had successfully led a double life. Professing to be completely rehabilitated and actively involved in the church, Joe secretly dealt crystal meth, even cooking the concoction in the boys' own home.

The church pastor, Jeb Bryant, was equally duped. Joe was his "success story," the one teen who had really converted and changed his ways. After living with Bryant and his wife, Joe had held down a construction job, participated in all of the church activities, and worked hard to be the type of person the pastor and his new friends thought him to be.

Only his girlfriend, Holly, knew the truth from the lie. The two had met through church activities and appeared to others to have a normal teenage relationship, off again and on again. No one realized, however, that the "off agains" were usually due to Joe flipping out on drugs or alcohol and hitting Holly. Despite his nights of wild binges, Joe always managed to show up for church on Sunday or to Josh's "accountability" Bible study.

Just two weeks earlier at his parole hearing, both Bryant and Josh had testified on Joe's behalf because they were so convinced of his sincere turnaround. Police records released after the murders revealed that Joe had been arrested several times for shoplifting, assault, and car theft when he was younger. It was the 1995 attack on another man that led to his final arrest. Halfway through his juvenile sentence, Joe had spent fourteen months in juvenile prison, a halfway house, and Jeb Bryant's foster home. Finally, Jeb Bryant had encouraged Josh to take Joe under his wing.

Josh not only invited Joe to room with him, but also helped him secure the construction job. They would carpool to work in the morning and host Bible studies in their home at night. Josh was committed to helping the young man who was to become his murderer.

Meanwhile, Joe's rocky relationship with Holly continued to sour. Holly moved four hundred miles away to the dorms at the University of Northern Colorado. Her social circle expanded, as did her interest in other men. When she tried to break off her relationship with Joe, he snapped.

For no apparent reason, Joe struck out at those who tried to help him. He shot all three roommates at point-blank range. When he arrived at Holly's dorm, hours later, he allegedly played a cassette tape to his girlfriend and declared, "This is the song I was listening to when I killed them. Now I'm going to kill you."

After a four-hour standoff with police, a sharpshooter killed Joe when he stood in front of the dormitory window. Crazy Joe had shot Holly once in the foot, but he did not harm her roommates.

The entire story seemed so senseless as Steve and Mary mourned the loss of their youngest child, a young man who held such promise for service in sharing the gospel and being a light in a dark world. Finding comfort in their family, they struggled with their pain and questions: *Was he afraid? Did he struggle?*

Yet as they mourned for their Josh, they sought solitude in their faith. They quickly recognized that Josh was in God's hands, not from their own prayers, but from his own. His diary revealed the depth of his commitment to being in God's will, his desire to live a godly life, and his interest in a deeper relationship with his Creator.

Steve and Mary came to the same conclusions for their own grieving. If they could trust God for everyday problems like money, business, illness, and the basic needs of raising a family, could they not also trust Him when facing such a tragedy? Should they not trust God even if unexpected, unwelcome violence burst into their lives, leaving them forever changed?

Silently and slowly, God's peace filled the Turville family. "The heavy stone lifted from our hearts," Steve later wrote, "and our minds were warmed with the assurance that God had His own perspective on Josh's death . . . and a purpose. We were wrapped in God's love as a baby is cuddled and pressed against his mother's breast. We felt safe. Our shoulders, which had been hunched against the pain for hours, were able to relax as we realized that nothing is beyond God's power. Nothing could happen to us or to Josh that was outside God's plan for our lives.

"You have a choice," Steve said. "You can look at this from the human perspective—your perspective—or you can look at it from God's perspective. I felt God say to me, *Josh is with me now, and although he is no longer with you, I'm still by your side. I'll meet your needs*. God's message to our aching hearts helped us as we took on the grim mission of the days to come."

Family members and friends called to share Bible verses with the Turvilles, including Romans 8:28: "All things work together for good to those who love God, to those who are the called according to His purpose," and verses 38–39, "Neither death nor life . . . nor any other created thing shall be able to separate us from the love of God."

As friends came to console, the media came to report. The news of the boys' murders consumed the local papers, which questioned the motives and analyzed the acts of the Good Samaritans. Reporters also came for photographs of an anguished family with clenched fists and angry remarks. One puzzled journalist commented to Steve and Mary, "Aren't you angry? You don't seem angry."

Anger that may consume other victims' families never came to the Turville home. Yes, the loss was great and their hearts ached, but they weren't angry. As they struggled to answer why, they realized Josh's life was not cut short. True, he died at an early age, but his life was complete as God had planned it. In spite of their loss and pain, they could not find it in their hearts to be angry.

As plans were made for a memorial service in their home church in Orange, Steve and Mary flew up to Bayfield to collect Josh's belongings, including his car. When Steve turned on the radio in the 4 Runner, out blasted the sound of the tape still in the player, which Joe had listened to on his dark drive to Greely.

Steve recoiled at the sound, not believing his ears. The ugliness of the music was an offensive look into the drug-induced, music-driven violence that had taken their son's life.

In brilliant contrast, the people of Bayfield and the church community opened their arms in spiritual support. Some came with tears and guilt. But Steve and Mary moved from person to person, comforting and calming the hearts of their son's friends.

At the memorial service, Jeb Bryant reminded everyone of Josh's heavenly reward. "Josh isn't here this morning to sing louder than all the rest of us put together," he said. "We know he is with the Lord, having the time of his life. We grieve, honestly and rightly. We mourn with those who mourn and we weep with those who weep, but we must also rejoice with those who rejoice, and we know that Josh is rejoicing right now."

He continued. "I spoke with Josh's dad the second day after all this happened. His dad said, 'God loaned us Josh for twenty years. This was a heart on loan from God.' "

The date of September 24 will forever represent a terrible loss. Yet the grace and peace Steve and Mary continue to experience after the violent death of their son was evident exactly one year after the murder. Although heartache still swelled and tears still flowed, there was peace. On that date, one year later, Steve's compassion to reach out mirrored that of his lost son's. He called another parent who lost a son that day—Crazy Joe Gallegos's mother.

"I just wanted to let you know that we offer our sympathy at the loss of your son a year ago today," Steve spoke softly, yet firmly.

On the other end there was a long pause, filled with hesitation. "I thought you'd want to forget about me and my son," was the defensive response.

"I couldn't do that," Steve calmly reassured, "even if I wanted to. I've chosen to remember your pain and loss as well as my own. Perhaps we can remind each other of happier times and of the comfort that God can bring to our hearts."

As their conversation continued, Steve went on to extend comfort. Finally he offered, "May I pray for you?"

And so he prayed: "Dear Jesus, we come to you today with heavy hearts. Neither one of us can change what is past. We can't predict the future either. But, Lord, we know that You are able to heal our hurting hearts and to take control of our uncertain futures. Your very presence with us today, on this anniversary day, gives us courage to look ahead to the year and know that our pain will lessen in the coming days, even though we will never stop caring about our loved ones who are gone. Please bless our families. In Jesus' name, Amen."

Steve heard a small sob on the other end and, with a few more words, he returned the receiver to the cradle.

The Turvilles attended seminars on grief and learned that it was normal to experience shock and numbness. They accepted the fact that anger, fear, and uncontrollable emotions could arise out of nowhere. Spells of guilt, panic, loneliness, and depression are normal in the rebuilding process. But not one seminar could teach them what they already knew, that which they had built their lives on—their foundation of faith.

Steve wrote these words as he sought solace in his faith:

The valley of the shadow of death is deep and not easy to climb out of. The challenges at first seem great, but as new relationships are built, new patterns of life are formed, and as new strengths are discovered, hope returns. As hope returns, we are strengthened. Eventually, our eyes turn toward others who are suffering. We realize that they need our help. After all, we have experienced what they are experiencing and we are surviving by God's grace. Perhaps they can find strength in Him too. Our hearts turn from our sorrow to others, and one day we will see this as the point at which we accepted our loss, and determined to go on with our lives.

The Savior of our souls will lead us out of the valley of the shadow of death to resur-

rection and life. He knows the way. He has walked this way before.

The Turvilles, heroes who turned their hurt into a halo, received my Scars into Stars award. So did June Scobee Rogers.

June Scobee Rogers

June Scobee Rogers truly demonstrates triumph of faith in the face of overwhelming defeat. From lowly beginnings through wrenching struggle, June has proven herself to be one of God's great souls.

June tells the complete story of her inspirational journey in *Silver Linings,* published by Peake Road in 1996. I wrote the foreword to that story, which touched my heart and renewed my conviction that God can turn all scars into stars. May her story here lead you beyond all your tribulations into triumph.

January 28, 1986, was a bitterly cold day on the coast of Florida. On the launch pad at Kennedy Space Center, the space shuttle Challenger glistened against the cold blue sky. Icicles hung from the wings and fuse-

lage of the orbiter. Inside, a crew of seven astronauts waited anxiously for their launch into space. One of them, the crew commander, Dick Scobee, was my husband.

Outside, in the crisp morning air, people gathered to watch. Television cameras stood ready, focused on the spacecraft that would take the crew of Challenger and a beloved schoolteacher into space. Their families waited too. We huddled together on the NASA observation deck. My children and I held on to each other for support and courage, waiting for the countdown that would launch their father into space.

As we waited, I gazed out across to the seashore where the shuttle was poised for liftoff. Memories came flooding back from the day before when my husband asked me to walk with him along that same sandy beach. I smiled to myself.

Thoughts carried me back to our afternoon walk, to the waves breaking on the shore, to the ocean spray and the unseasonably cool weather. Dick pulled me close to him as we stepped out onto the wet sand, leaving behind only a faint track of footprints at the ocean's edge.

The salty sea breeze, the sounds of hun-

gry seagulls, and the drifting bubbles at our feet were restful images. Most of all, we enjoyed the steady, rhythmic sounds of the ocean waves crashing upon the shore then gently flowing back and lazily churning under and into the next wave.

We had walked up the coast until we could see out across the sandy marshland to the shuttle cloaked in the misty air. We stopped and gazed longingly. Finally, Dick spoke, "That's home away from home for the next week for seven of us . . . It's going to be crowded!"

We smiled, then turned to the sea and stared out at the horizon, across the Atlantic Ocean. Dick hummed a familiar tune about a sailor on the sea saying farewell, then turned to me and sang part of it aloud. We embraced. I felt his love and appreciated his tender words and hung on to them for a long, long while. We teased. He took my hand as we turned to walk back to the beach house where the others were waiting.

The next morning, all the families of the astronauts met at NASA headquarters. We came together watching and waiting for the launch of the Challenger. Finally, the countdown for Shuttle Flight 51-L began. The solid rocket boosters (SRBs) ignited. We cheered, and then the shuttle carrying its precious cargo lifted off the pad. Only a few anxious moments left. We watched in silence as our loved ones climbed the sky sunward. Their craft from the distance seemed to sit atop a great plume of smoke. The floor shook with the sheer raw power of the millions of pounds of thrust.

My son lovingly and protectively put his arms around me and his sister. As I reached to help my daughter with the baby . . . the unspeakable happened.

Standing there together, watching with all the world, we saw the shuttle rip apart. The SRBs went screaming off on their own separate paths, and the orbiter with our loved ones exploded in the cold blue sky. Like our hearts it shattered into a million pieces.

In stunned silence, we looked to each other for answers, for information, for hope? No words came, no answers, only glances. I saw the pain in my children's eyes. If only I could turn back that clock, if I could stop time. I had no power, no answers. "O God! It can't be," I whispered to myself. "I won't believe it. Why did you let this happen? Not my husband. Not his flight! Not his crew! My friends! I let these people down. I encouraged the flight. I explained away the risks. Why, God? Why them? Why us? Why me? This is not what happens at a shuttle launch."

My son took my arm to support me. My legs felt numb. They wobbled clumsily. I stumbled. Finally, I spoke out loud, "What about the others?" I asked. "Who's helping the children?" Oh no! Dear God, all those children!

Minutes later, we were on a bus to crew quarters. My memory fails here. It's all a blur, like a nightmare that you try to piece together but the fit isn't rational. I prayed for a miracle. Just let them survive, dear God. My head knew they were dead; my heart did not.

At a stoplight, I turned my rigid body to the window to look out. Cars were everywhere, stopped on the streets, on the curbs and sidewalks. People embraced one another, perhaps friends, maybe strangers. Some stood outside their cars, heads resting on their arms across their doors; others sat sobbing into their hands at the steering wheel. A wave of shock jolted across the land and through the people and around the world.

My thoughts careened to the others, and always back to myself. My life as it had been, the path Dick and I traveled together for twenty-six years, had reached its end, and the path that reached into the future with us at each other's side was gone. From that moment, I would be changed—a different person—alone. And Dick's mission, his dreams, his life, his friends—gone. They were doing the best of things for their country, pioneers all, crossing the frontier into tomorrow.

The bus delivered us to the door of crew quarters, where NASA officials gave us the tragic news. "All crew members are dead. They could not have survived." No hope, no miracle, no chance. I left the others to slip away into Dick's private room so I could be alone to cry out in rage. Instead, I fell to my knees to pray.

I wept for my husband, for myself and family, for our friends with us, and for those who worked for NASA, and the contractors, pioneers themselves, who supported and believed in space exploration. What a tragedy! What a terrible loss to humanity!

That night, NASA arranged for the families to return to our homes in Houston. Friends met us at the airport. They held us in their arms, drove us to our homes, and took our relatives into their homes. Where there was confusion, they brought order. They made arrangements for us; they protected us.

I walked; somehow I put one foot in front of the other. I walked and feigned strength, but inside I, too, was dying, stunned, incomprehensible. Worst of all, I thought myself gone—the nurturer, caretaker, provider couldn't even help my own suffering children. I mourned the loss of my husband who was my partner in life, my best friend, and my companion. And I mourned the loss of myself—different, changed, a widow. I choked on the word.

My feelings of guilt, both irrational and justified, kept crashing through my head like a thunderbolt. Why didn't I stop them from flying? Why hadn't I prepared the children better? I grew weary of self-recrimination. Helplessly, I cried. Purposefully, I prayed for strength and forgiveness. Finally, I slept.

Memorial services, arrangements for visitors, decisions were mechanically made in the following weeks. I began to acknowl-

edge but not accept their deaths. They had gone on to a better place. Their bodies were buried at sea, but they were here with us—angels among us, guiding us.

Weeks later, we learned that their bodies had been found, nearly three months after their deaths. Disbelief, pain, and now, anger returned. Our loss was so public. Was there no sacred privacy? We had buried them, or at least, I had rationalized to myself that they were at peace. Now the anguish returned along with the media to my door, on the phone. Questions, some sensitive, some not. Regrets, guilt, sorrow returned like a giant crashing wave, knocking me down.

I was angry with God for letting this happen. The energy used for anger, hate, and grief were sapping me of my life. If you won't take me, I begged, then give me strength . . . to live this life, to help me solve these problems, to overcome these feelings of guilt.

That moment, I became like a child again. I turned my life over to God. God was in control—not I. For the first time in my life since grappling with losses in my childhood, I relinquished complete control to God. A joyous Spirit challenged me to live, to ac-

cept my problems, to discover new joy in a new life. My faith was renewed.

Though I was alone in my house, I didn't feel alone. No longer the master of my own fate, the simple innocence of the child I once knew told me that God was with me, in control. The pressure, the anger, the pain, and the guilt slowly drained from my body. A part of me died, but a stronger, more centered, saner self was born.

I stared in the mirror and, through different eyes, I saw a new person. My cheeks were flushed pink like the little girl I once knew. The numbness I had known for months subsided. Piece by piece, I became more alive.

I stepped outside on the shady, green lawn and thanked the early morning light for chasing away the darkness. I looked at my hands, my arms. The tense, tight feeling was gone. I was more alert, more conscious of life around me. For the first time in months, I felt the tingle of a breeze floating across my skin. A ray of sunlight felt warm across my back.

A single golden daffodil bent forward as if to welcome me to new life. Tears rained down my cheeks—not tears of sorrow or self-pity, not this time. Lord knows I'd shed enough of those. No, these were tears of joy for rebirth to live out this life with my children and their children on a new journey, in a new direction, along whatever path God unfolded for me.

During the month of May, seven families arranged funerals, services, and burials for their loved ones. Each family planned according to their religion or family tradition or loved one's request. Protestant, Catholic, Jewish, Buddhist. Some private, others public.

I talked with our children and Dick's parents and our pastor. We chose to honor the man who relished his privacy. A modest headstone, symbolic of the plain and simple life he most wanted, was placed at his grave site near the Challenger Astronauts Monument at Arlington National Cemetery.

We also arranged a service for the more public figure—the astronaut, the military man who loved and served his country well. Friends and family joined us for this more formal ceremony. They walked with us from the chapel to the grave site to pay their last respects. "Taps" was played as I placed flowers on Dick's grave, located across from the Unknown Soldier, on a spread of grassy green, beneath shade trees.

He's not there, though. On January 28 he and his six crewmates climbed a golden beam of light sunward to the heavens to touch the stars. Instead they "put out their hands and touched the face of God."

The families came together in my home, sitting around the coffee table in my living room, to decide together how we could respond to our loss and help our nation to heal. The world knew that seven Challenger astronauts died, but they were more than astronauts. They were our husbands and wife, fathers and mother, brothers and sister. The world knew how they had died. We wanted the world to know how they had lived.

Their mission became our mission. We named it the Challenger Center for Space Science Education. On mighty wings, it would rise out of the ashes to create a living tribute to the Challenger Seven. We asked our team of volunteers if we could create simulated space flight for children that allowed lessons in science and math. Could this experience provide opportunities for children to problem solve and work together as a team on their own simulated mission?

At times great dark clouds of frustration would block our path, but unexpected glimmers of hope would light our way . . . really answers to prayers.

And the team grew once we announced our mission. From children who sent their nickels, dimes, and pennies (one sent his tooth fairy money) to the elderly who still believed in the great American dream, to leaders in government, business, and education.

Our circle of friends grew until the ripples (like those created from a stone cast upon a pond) reached across America and around the world. And, most important, into the classrooms of students and teachers still waiting for their lessons from space.

President Bush in his remarks at the Challenger Center National Awards Dinner, in 1989, pledged his continuing support:

"The mission of Challenger Center is to spark in our young people an interest—and a joy—in science. A spark that can change their lives and help make American enterprise the envy of the world." He concluded, "The fallen astronauts have taken their place

in the heavens—so that America can take its place in the stars."

Today, students and their teachers throughout North America travel to one of the thirty-five Challenger Learning Center sites on a different kind of field trip . . . one that takes them outside the boundaries of our planet and right back home into their classroom textbooks.

For me, lessons we learned were not those planned for by the Teacher in Space mission. Instead there were lessons of forgiveness, overcoming adversity, problem solving, forfeiting control to God, and the opportunity to welcome new life through a closer walk with our Savior, Jesus Christ.

Greatest of all, I learned lessons about love—the beautiful power of love that can cause a magnificent phoenix to rise up out of the ashes of a tragedy.

Franklin D. Roosevelt once said, "We cannot always build the future for our youth, but we can build our youth for the future." That's what all those great people accomplished when they created Challenger Center. They made a difference. They touched the future not only for the crew members of Challenger, who set out to explore, to inspire, to learn, to teach, but also for generations of children who will reach out to the stars and work hard to see their dreams come true.

The greatest lesson—God's love—reaches into the future; it has no limits and knows no boundaries. It can change the complexion of the universe or the color of our world, and turn tribulations into triumphs.

Today June Scobee Rogers lives in Chattanooga, Tennessee, on the side of a mountain that overlooks the winding Tennessee River. She lives there with her husband, Don Rogers, a retired army general whom she met several years after the Challenger accident during an Easter sunrise service at Arlington National Cemetery. She makes regular visits to the network of Challenger Learning Center sites across the country and delights in moments shared with any one of her nine grandchildren.

June Scobee Rogers received my Scars into Stars award. So did Art Linkletter, another hero who turned his hurt into a halo.

"There is a light in this world, a healing spirit more powerful than any darkness we may encounter. We sometimes lose sight of this force when there is suffering, and too much pain. Then suddenly, the spirit will emerge through the lives of ordinary people who hear a call and answer in extraordinary ways."

—Mother Teresa

Art Linkletter

The night of October 4, 1969, will linger in Art Linkletter's memory forever. It is there when he wakes up in the morning and when he goes to sleep at night. When he stands to speak to almost any of the hundreds of audiences he addresses every year, that date is fresh on his mind.

It's almost as if it were yesterday. And in a way, October 4, 1969 was yesterday for Art Linkletter, so vivid is his recollection of the events that transpired that day.

On October 4, 1969, a twenty-year-old girl, whom many considered to be an up-and-coming young star in Hollywood, jumped to her death from the kitchen window of her sixth-story apartment.

The girl was found to have been under the influence of the drug LSD. The girl was Diane Linkletter, Art Linkletter's youngest child.

Art was at the United States Air Force Academy in Colorado Springs, Colorado, with his wife, Lois, preparing to speak to the cadets about the evils inherent in an affluent society. There was a telephone call, and the caller refused to hang up, demanding to talk with Art. He identified himself as Robert Linkletter, Art's son.

Robert had received a telephone call from Diane earlier that evening. She was panicky, screaming something about losing her mind. Robert attempted to calm her, and when she hung up, he ran to his car and raced to her apartment.

He got there too late!

And now he faced the herculean task of telling his father and mother that their daughter, and his sister, was dead.

Art and Lois were stunned and saddened, each experiencing a dozen emotions all at once. His speech was abruptly cancelled, and he and Lois hurried back to Los Angeles and to the rest of their family.

At first, the full realization of what had happened was too much for Art to bear. How could his daughter have committed suicide? How could she have even used drugs at all? Drugs were used by "bad" kids, or kids who came from broken homes or who were spoiled by uncaring parents. This was not Diane. The Linkletter family—Art, Lois, and their five children—were all close. They did things together, went on vacations together, and went to church together. Theirs was a happy, God-fearing home, not like the homes of some other Hollywood stars they knew.

Art was devastated. Again and again he wondered how something like this could happen to his family. He had worked so hard all his life to get where he was—from the day he was found as a baby on the doorstep of a Baptist minister, who later adopted him, through his childhood, his early radio days, and on to the days when programs such as *House Party, People Are Funny*, and *Hollywood Talent Scout* made Art Linkletter one of the biggest radio and television personalities in the country. Throughout this time he had clung to the belief that right and wrong were two separate, easily identified entities and that using drugs was definitely wrong.

Today, many years after that terrible day in 1969, Art can recall that there were signs Diane was engaging in some occasional experiments with drugs, but he had chosen to ignore them.

"I couldn't conceive it," he told me. "As parents we don't want to believe that it can happen to our kids, and that's often our biggest problem. I figured that with four other kids I knew all about raising children. You develop a pattern of comfortable conformity, and you're not prepared for any difference that might arise."

After the initial numbness wore off, anger set in. Seething anger, coupled with a tremendous sense of loss, had an effect on Art's ability to think and act clearly.

Art was boiling mad and he stayed that way. He declared an official war on drug users and pushers, especially pushers. These people had killed his daughter by giving her drugs, and he was going to get revenge.

By his own admission Art is not a full-fledged pacifist, but anyone who knows him can readily tell that Art is not someone who enjoys or even entertains thoughts of hurting others. He himself knows that to strike back while in the midst of anger often produces the wrong results.

But now he found himself unable to accept his own advice. The pushers roamed the streets, selling their wares to America's young people, selling drugs to people like Diane, and he was out to put a stop to it. So intense were his hatred and anger and fear that at a closed meeting of the directors of the National Association of Manufacturers (NAM), in Boca Raton, Florida, Art threatened to kill another human being.

The object of this hatred was a psychologist, teacher, and self-styled guru who preached that LSD was good for people and, using the drug, built a pseudoreligion that attracted thousands of youthful followers.

At the NAM meeting Art was asked his observations on the drug-abuse problem. Without mincing words, Art launched into an attack on that man, ending his tirade by saying, "If I ever get my hands on him, so help me God, I'll kill him."

During all this anger, however, Art

made one decision that would have a lasting effect on him and his family and would send shock waves through the entertainment colony at Hollywood.

He decided to tell the truth!

Hollywood personalities are taught to always put forth a good face. Life is sweet and happy in Tinseltown. Nothing ever goes wrong, or if it does, the public is never to hear about it. That's what press agents are for, to sugarcoat everything and divert inquiries that might lead to unpleasant revelations.

Art decided to forget all that and tell the truth. He told his story to the nation's press, told the country that his daughter had not died from an accident but had jumped to her death because she was under the influence of drugs.

The reaction was immediate and somewhat frightening.

Rumormongers from scandal sheets immediately pounced on the story and blew it out of proportion. To listen to them, one would think that the whole Linkletter family had been knocked to its knees or that all the children were heavily into drugs. The columnists played on the emotions Art and his family were feeling, writing again and again about their loss. The family's private sorrow suddenly became public.

All that, though, had been anticipated and expected. Art had been in the entertainment business for forty years, so he knew what to expect when something of this nature became public knowledge. But what Art didn't expect was the outpouring of letters from families all across the country who had suffered the same terrible tragedy. Many sympathized and asked him what had gone wrong, where had they failed their children? Others wrote that they knew their kids were involved in drugs and might one day suffer the same fate as Diane. What could they do to prevent it?

But along with these letters came messages from false sympathizers, those who pretended to share Art's grief only to use it as a way, hopefully, to get Art to endorse their programs, which they felt would eradicate drug use in no time.

This insult on top of injury only inflamed and confused Art more.

One day a letter arrived that began much like all the other letters. It, too, expressed sympathy at Diane's death. But this letter went on and asked Art to think through her death and seek from it a purpose, a meaning.

This letter was from Dr. Norman Vincent Peale, and it had a profound effect on Art's life. Dr. Peale urged Art to shape something positive from the ashes of Diane's tragedy. It was a calling card to begin a campaign against drugs, which Art decided to do. To this day, Art believes that God, through Dr. Peale's letter, touched him that day and brought a sense of purpose back into his life.

He had already begun his campaign against drug abuse in this country. But Art's story was far from over.

When he first began speaking on drug abuse, Art's message was that stricter laws for pushers and better educational programs—to show students exactly what would happen if they began experimenting with drugs—were necessary. Police needed to be given full rein, with permission to arrest or club someone on the head if need be.

Art believed that drug abuse was a black-and-white situation. The kids who used drugs were bad; those who didn't were good. It was the accepted belief at the time, and Art was its foremost proponent.

But as he moved about the country talking to high school and college students, seeing their reactions, listening to their viewpoints, Art came to the realization that the issue of drug abuse was not black-and-white, but rather varying shades of gray. There was no quick, easy solution to the problem, no flip phrase that would sum up the answer in five words or less.

It took eight months for Art to overcome his anger and force himself to take a long, objective look at drug abuse. He found that it wasn't always the "bad" kids who were involved with drugs; normal, intelligent kids admitted to smoking marijuana or experimenting with hard drugs.

Parents are often to blame, either because they fail to discipline or even care about their children, or because they go to the other extreme and are too harsh, too unbending.

But sometimes parents are not to blame. Peer pressure often forces a youngster into drug experimentation. The need to be accepted is strong in young people, and often this acceptance is granted only after drug use becomes involved.

Art was able to channel the energy that he had previously devoted to sustaining his anger into learning all he could about drugs and drug users, why they took drugs and where they got them. He visited drug rehabilitation centers, spent time working as a volunteer on crisis hot lines. He began realizing that his previous throw-them-into-jail stance did little to solve drug abuse.

Art has continued his war against drug abuse, but on a much different level than before. He has served on the President's Advisory Council on Drug Abuse and was president of the National Coordinating

Council on Drug Abuse Education and Information. In 1971 he addressed the General Assembly of the United Nations on drug abuse. He wrote a book, *Drugs at My Doorstep*, which detailed his experiences and quickly became a best seller. He continues a hectic schedule today, traveling more than a quarter of a million miles each year speaking to various groups, usually about drug abuse.

Wherever he goes, parents ask him for advice in dealing with their children who are often involved with drugs.

Art's answer is simple.

"Attempt to understand the situation as unemotionally as you can. Discuss the situation with your kids," Art advises. "Don't react too strongly. Hear your child out. Don't shut him or her off with an angry display. You'll often find that the problem is a mixture of a lot of things: peer pressure, a desire to be happy all the time. It's a different level of growing up."

Since I have had the pleasure of appearing on programs with Art, and have had him as a guest more than once on our television program, I know from personal observations that the tragedy of losing a daughter still weighs heavily on his mind. When discussing it, he becomes quieter, a bit withdrawn perhaps, but never to the point of refusing to talk about it. He decided many years ago to tell the truth, and though the truth still hurts, it must be told and retold and retold.

A side effect of Art's decision to go public with the tragedy and disclose the real truth was the reverberations it sent throughout the Hollywood community. That decision changed the way many Hollywood stars treat the public. Now they are less afraid of telling the truth, less afraid of showing that they are, after all, human, and those humans have problems, sometimes serious problems. The revelations of Carol Burnett and the battle she underwent to free her daughter from the effect of drugs is but one example.

"My speaking up has given all the rest the strength to speak out," Art told me. "If we take the bows for the good things, we should also show the weaker side of things as well."

The experience of Diane's death has changed Art and his family. For one thing, it has brought an already close family closer. As for Art, he's noticed some changes within himself, too.

"I've become more compassionate, understanding, tolerant, religious, and loving. When you see as many people hurting as I have, you have to develop these feelings. Now happiness and satisfaction are the most important things in the world to me."

Art's message to anyone who is confronted with the task of picking up the pieces and putting them back together after a devastating tragedy is simple. He tells them: "God has a reason for everything. Sometimes it's hard to find or understand His reason, but we must accept the fact that He always has a reason. We must search for His reason, and then we must set out to turn our scars into stars."

"There is no grief that I have experienced that has come close to my grief over the loss of our child. Throughout our months and years of grieving, faith has been the redeeming force that has enabled us to bear the pain and continue to live in victory. The very process of grief is given to us by a loving heavenly Father. God uses grief to heal us, strengthen us in our faith, and cause us to grow in our relationship with Him."

—ZIG ZIGLAR

SPEAKER AND AUTHOR

10
There's Life Beyond Hope!

So this is where every hurt leads each suffering soul. And what is *this*? A place called *decision-making time*.

You must come to a time and place where you are alone. All alone. Even your O.E.F. (one essential friend) is not with you.

Solitude. Welcome to this rich and risky, rare but rewarding, moment. Do not be afraid. You are all alone, but you are not abandoned. You are in a spiritual place where you can think and pray alone.

Here your emotional world can break loose and be free from your limiting hang-ups, and holdups, which have been mental barricades blocking you from making life's most important personal decision.

And what is that?!

It's a decision to become a believer in God. *Come to the edge,* He is saying to you now.

It's decision-making time.

Three basic options are open to you and

to every human alive today, tomorrow, or a thousand years from now.

These three options are to become an atheist, to become an agnostic, or to become a believer.

THE THREE OPTIONS

Yes, it's decision-making time. To ignore decision making by accident or intention is the most unintelligent and foolhardy choice you can make in the catalog of disastrous human choices.

"Why," I asked Mother Teresa, "don't people choose to believe in God when it makes them feel so good to touch the edge of divine love that's been alive in this spiritual universe for all of eternity?"

Her answer, in one word: "Distractions."

If you are reading these pages in private, you may be saved right now from secular distractions.

Enjoy the peace.

The sublime solitude.

The divine aloneness.

Prepare here and now to make life's greatest decision, to choose from the three options before you: atheism, agnosticism, or belief in God.

ATHEISM

An atheist is a believer in nothing. Know this, if you choose to decide to be an atheist. You become a brash believer in nothing. Nihilism reigns here. To the true atheist there is no God and no life after death.

To the atheist there is no immortality of the soul. There is no eternal life, no heaven or hell, no ultimate justice or appropriate reward.

To choose atheism is to close the door of your thinking to any possibility that a Supreme Being ever did or does exist. To choose atheism you become a super impossibility thinker and confess your faith in ultimate nothingness.

The atheist declares:

- "Believe in God? Impossible!"
- "Believe in a higher intelligence than humans? Impossible!"
- "Believe in eternal life? No way!"

An atheist negates all evidence of the religious history of humans and all evidence in nature that a creative intelligence was there in eternity before this earth and this cosmos existed. Atheism negates all possibility of a Supreme Being, a higher, holier power. If you choose to be or become an atheist, know this: You will join the ranks of ultimate negative thinkers.

Then you will take your place with the world's supreme impossibility thinkers who will not (yes, it's a matter of will—it's a decision) believe in anything as long as their questions remain unanswered.

Would you really call this intelligence?

I repeat again the words of the great American physicist Dr. Edward Teller, "Become scientists, and all your life remember these words: *I don't know*." Humble science always leaves the door open to possibilities that may be unprovable realities!

The terrible tragedy of atheism is what it does to personhood. One's personality and behavioral performance will undebatably be conditioned, shaped, and directed by his or her decision to be an atheist.

What kind of a person is shaped by the core mind-set of an atheist? For starters let's look at Madalyn Murray O'Hair, one of the most famous atheists of modern times.

She founded the national group American Atheists Inc. in the 1960s.

Where is she today? We don't know. She mysteriously disappeared along with her son and granddaughter. According to the *New York Times*, the three have not been seen or heard from since September 1995.

But her diaries were found and have been auctioned off to pay a large IRS debt. According to the *Times* article, O'Hair was obsessed with money, power, and her waistline. Her New Year's goals for 1973 included "Get a mink coat, a Cadillac. And humiliate Billy Graham for money."

Perhaps the biggest insights her diaries reveal are the thoughts and delusions of an unhappy person. Every road takes us somewhere, so where did Madalyn Murray O'Hair's road of atheistic belief take her? In her diary entry dated October 9, 1956, she wrote, "What is the matter with hating? It is treated as a leper among the emotions. Why in the hell should we go around exuding sweetness and light?"

Atheism shapes impossibility thinkers into personalities where:

- Healthy humility is often replaced by arrogant elitism.
- Creative wonderment is replaced by the cold cynicism represented in this little ditty:

  Twinkle, twinkle little star
  I know exactly what you are.
  An incandescent ball of gas
  Condensing to a solid mass.

- Emotional fertility is replaced by spiritual barrenness.

In atheism something sick and sad happens in the subconscious. The womb of human emotions—which by nature is so potentially warm, friendly, fertile, and fruitful—is made frigid to the intrusion of warm and wonderful feelings. And this frigidity leads to inevitable infertility. The heart becomes barren, unable to conceive and create positive human emotions.

Early students of anthropology, psychology, and theology had to come up with a word to describe the healthy, positive, ebullient personality. They came up with a word that is the same in both English and Russian; they tapped into Greek for the purest and most precise definition. They took the

Greek word *en* (in) and *Theos* (God), and the new word became *enthusiasm!* Atheism and genuine, full-blooming enthusiasm do not naturally coexist.

My most insightful experience with atheism occurred in 1989, when I became the first foreigner to be invited to dialogue with the head of Russian television, who admitted to me, "We are atheists and have used television and academia to teach atheism. . . . But after seventy years of atheism, we are coming to discover that there are some positive emotions possible in human beings that are only realized through religion."

To choose to become an atheist is to choose to live painfully and cynically without hope—now and forever.

Think! Where does this road called atheism lead? To spiritual and emotional death! But you are free to choose *life*—abundant, fertile, and eternal!

AGNOSTICISM

Agnosticism is another option. "I can't be sure if there is a God or not, so I'll play it safe and leave the door open to either possibility. I'm not going to make a decision." That's the mind-set of the agnostic.

Here's the contradiction the agnostic must live with: Indecision is a decision too.

So the choice is yours. And agnosticism cannot possibly be the right decision.

A dear friend, Larry King, is in a league of his own. His daily television talk show on CNN is the only call-in talk show that can be seen globally. Anybody who is anybody might be seen and heard on his far-flung program.

I, too, have guests every week on my global television program, the *Hour of Power*. As I wrote this chapter, I had the honor of interviewing Larry King on the publication of his latest book, *Powerful Prayers*. His coauthor was Rabbi Katsof. Because I wrote the foreword, Larry's appearance in the Sunday morning taping of my television program was appropriate, even though he called himself an agnostic.

"That's my decision," he explained, adding, "I don't have the answers to the questions I raise. That's why I've chosen not to be a committed believer, like my coauthor, Rabbi Katsof."

Larry added, "The atheist has chosen to

have faith that there is no God . . . and the believer has chosen to believe there is a God," he said. "The agnostic says, 'I don't know. I'm not taking sides.' "

Then he shot out the sentence, "Either the atheist or the believer is wrong! As an agnostic I can't be wrong."

"But, Larry," I answered, "just because you're not wrong doesn't mean you're right. Either the atheist or the believer is right! And so you can be sure that as long as you evade and avoid a choice, you are for sure missing the right decision! And that could be terribly wrong."

Being "not wrong" is not good enough! You can be "not wrong" and still be no good for anything. A field that never grows weeds doesn't do anything wrong. It just isn't doing what it should be doing right—growing food!

The decision is really simple. Being a believer is the choice that brings with it unlimited positive possibilities! As a believer, I tap into the hidden powers that total commitment releases. I am turned into a person who focuses on creative possibilities. I am shaped into a person with a mental attitude that's open to countless creative options!

In our interview Larry King said that the

difference between us was that I had taken a "leap of faith."

"Oh, it's a commitment," I responded. "A commitment to be a believer in God and in Jesus and in the Bible. Because it makes sense."

"Therefore," Larry concluded, "are you saying that your faith is an intelligent commitment you choose because it makes more sense than choosing not to be a believer?"

"That's right!" I said. "For when you have made a leap of faith, to use your words, Larry, it's awesome to see the fantastic possibilities, even in the face of hurt, pain, and injustice."

> *Faith—it's a decision not a debate!*
> *Faith—it's a commitment not an argument!*

There remains so much hurt in humanity that I cannot understand, but I don't allow the mysteries of suffering to rob me of my positive faith in a good God.

"How," Larry King asked, "can you explain the horror that happens to humans—if you believe in God?!"

"I can't explain it," I answered. "I'm not

God, so I don't know and I'm not expected to understand it!"

Later I thought about all the people I've known who kept their faith in God even though they suffered horrific pain. You've read many of their stories in this book. Remember Elie Weisel and Viktor Frankl, who lived through Hitler's Holocaust? Another Holocaust survivor who kept his faith in God was Benjamin Hirsch.

Benjamin was a child during the Holocaust. He tells an insightful story about Baal Shem-Tov, the great rabbi who is considered to be the founder of the Hasidic movement. Baal Shem-Tov was standing high on a hill with a couple of his students, looking down at the town where his school was. Suddenly, a group of cossacks on horseback attacked the town.

As the rabbi saw many of his students along with the men, women, and children of the town being slaughtered, Baal Shem-Tov looked up to heaven and said, "Oh, if only I were God."

One of his students said, with astonishment, "But, Master, if you were God, what would you do differently?"

The reply was, "If I were God, I would do

nothing differently. If I were God, I would understand."[1]

We tend to expect to be inspired through reading the Bible, or through creative and inspirational work, but we don't expect to be inspired through pain and hurt. Many of us, like Hirsch, sense a mysterious stirring within us. It is a stirring that tells us that something larger than us is at work, that something is filling our spirits and inspiring us to press on.

We will never be able to understand a gun pointed at an infant's head, or the loss and cruelty experienced during the Holocaust. But, like Hirsch, we may be able to understand—in hindsight or as it happens—that God is present in our blessings and in our trials.

We read in the book of Job that "there is a spirit in man, and the breath of the Almighty gives him understanding." To know this is to know our limits as human beings. We do not, on our own, have God's understanding. We do not have His vision. When we become inspired, we are granted a moment of hearing or seeing what we ordinarily do not hear or see. We are lifted up above our grief and empowered to feel the halo coming out of the hurt.

> *To the atheist,*
> *there's no hope beyond life.*
> *To the believer,*
> *There's life beyond hope.*

Come to the edge, God says to the agnostic! *Come to the edge! And let me push you, and you will fly!*

That is why I have chosen to live my life on the edge! And He pushed me! And I flew—the past seventy years—as a believer. It's been, beyond any question, the right decision for me and will be for you too!

The decision is yours. Atheist? Agnostic? or Believer? Since this is the most important decision of your life, certainly pray about it! Even if you don't believe in God.

My final word to Larry King was, "Larry, read the prayer for agnostics. I wrote it. You published it. It's in your book of *Powerful Prayers.* But if you read it here—in my church, you will go on record as having knowingly prayed your first public prayer on Dr. Schuller's *Hour of Power*." I opened his book to the page. He read it silently, then turned to me and said, "Okay! Here goes my first public prayer."

> Dear God, I don't know where to start. I'm going to try to talk to You. I don't know if I'm getting through. If I'm on the right track, let me hear You. And if I'm not on the right track, let me hear You.

I urge every doubtful reader to pray this prayer. Give God a chance to help you find a positive faith.

BECOME A BELIEVER

The final option, the most positive choice, is to become a believer in some superior spiritual intelligence that is good and beautiful.

The believer makes a decision to believe in a God who is creative, intelligent, affectionate, and life affirming, even when he cannot explain or understand God. It's the ultimate level of possibility thinking. Call it the leap of faith from a solid, spiritually-scientific platform.

One of the most memorable experiences in my life happened in Japan. A group of

Japanese students confronted me after a lecture on possibility thinking. (They were interested that I was a member of the Board of Directors of the American Institute of Architecture.)

"If there's really a supreme intelligence called God—and if humans were designed to be spiritual animals created in His image and engineered to be capable of imagining the existence of God—then why," they asked, "didn't God make that a scientific fact, instead of leaving it a mystery to be grasped by religious faith?"

"You must understand the architecture of human personality," I answered. "Faith is a scientific reality. Faith is not abnormal and unnatural. In reality, faith is the fulfillment of spiritual facilities designed and engineered to evolve this animal called man into a fully developed creature called a spiritual human being.

"The architecture of human personality is engineered around the basic faith principle. The purpose of our personality is to be an instrument of creativity. Creativity can take raw materials called ideas and invent products and services that can benefit humanity. Ideas interface and interconnect in the same way that walls, floors, and ceilings join to create structures or buildings."

For instance, in architecture the first concept in design is to choose the engineering principle. What power will span the space to join walls and support the roof? Early Egyptian architecture chose pillars and tall columns—tall enough and close enough to each other to support beams cut from large, long stones. The results were buildings that were narrow and limited in space and spanning.

The advent of steel allowed the birth of awesome structures. High-rise buildings became a possibility. Massive open spaces, covered by a single ceiling, were possible with steel beams connecting widely spaced walls.

What columns were to Egyptian architecture, what steel beams are to skyscrapers, that's what faith is to the architecture of the human personality. Faith is the "spiritual steel beams" connecting ideas that join to open up the possibilities of human creativity, which makes us capable of love, trust, and hope.

Yes, faith is the basic engineering principle in the ultimate creative development of human personality.

Without faith, we humans evolve into spiritually deprived creatures. Pathetically, we never dare to discover and develop our vast potential as spiritually creative persons! Without the empowerment of this faith engineering principle, our human imaginations may never envision their awesome potential.

In short, life without faith, is life lived without hope! And in essence, without faith, the human personality is devoid of energy and enthusiasm.

Now we can see what the seventy-year Russian experiment with atheism in the social laboratory has proved. Life without the faith principle limits the development of human potential.

Jesus Christ said it so well: "I have come that you may have life, and have it more abundantly" (John 10:10).

FAITH MORE ABUNDANT

The cobblestone streets of Sicily promised romance and rest to my wife and me following a busy, but dynamic, trip to Italy for a mission conference. We looked forward to dining in the quaint restaurants overlooking the Mediterranean. We relished the warmth of the sun-drenched skies. What was supposed to be a few days of work mingled with history and relaxation ended abruptly. Arvella, my wife of forty-seven years, came out of the bathroom with a painful look on her face. "Bob, I don't feel good," she said. "I'm really sick."

Her face, her voice, and her terrible indigestion coupled with the surging pain shooting down her left arm alarmed me. I had had a mild heart attack only four months earlier, and I insisted she take one of my nitroglycerin pills.

The cobblestone streets now produced a jarring ambulance ride to a crowded, dingy emergency room filled with a foreign tongue and suspicious stares. Throughout the frightening transfer and the confusion and loneliness of being the only woman in an all-male ward, my wife found comfort and peace from her childhood faith.

The extent of her heart attack was unknown. She would need to wait eight days in Italy before her condition stabilized enough to be flown back home where she would undergo a six-artery bypass surgery.

In the days and weeks to come, she clung to her positive faith in Jesus Christ.

Arvella's heart surgery was a complete success—but not without a serious setback. In the early morning hours following her first night in recovery, bleeding began that would not stop. The surgeon and doctor on staff tried to stop the bleeding—all without success.

Arvella remembers one doctor struggling with the suction tube in her chest. He looked extremely worried. "I can't reach the blood clots. We need to open her again," she heard him say. Then he asked, "Has the blood arrived?"

After one painful hour she was rushed back into surgery. That meant that her still-fragile body, swollen from being pulled apart, rib cage and all, would be reopened to hopefully solve the problem of bleeding and blood clots.

Meanwhile, exhausted from a day of sitting in a hospital waiting room, I had gone to bed that night praising God for a successful surgery, yet prayerful that my wife would recover on schedule. Unfortunately, when the doctors tried to call me early the next morning, I missed the call. Arvella went back into surgery without my being there.

"When I heard the words *blood clot* I knew I was dying," Arvella said. "I was filled with a true indescribable peace and presence of Jesus Christ. The words that immediately came to me were His words: 'Do not be afraid; only believe.' In my mind I kept repeating those words, and I was prepared to meet my God—Jesus Christ. It was a most beautiful experience."

> *"Have courage for the great sorrows of life and patience for the small ones; and when you have laboriously accomplished your daily task, go to sleep in peace. God is awake."*
>
> —VICTOR HUGO
> AUTHOR (1802–1885)

What is so sensational about a positive faith in a caring and compassionate God is the honesty of it all! Believers are not Pollyanna people. Faith is reality thinking. It says, "Hey! I'm going to walk through the valley of the shadow of death."

Secular people don't want to talk about

the subject. They don't even want to think about the cemeteries. Historic believers are the reality thinkers. We know we will all go through the valley of the shadow of death. We are ready for it.

The psalmist was the super reality thinker. "Yes, though I [whatever my age] *walk* through the valley of the shadow of death, I will fear no evil." Just think of those words—not crawl, not creep, not cringe, but *walk* upright.

Walk. "Yes, though I walk *through* the valley." *Through*, not to or into, but *through* it. God doesn't send us *to* the valley, He walks with us *through* the valley. This is part of the process of living, and death is no problem as long as you are not afraid. The psalmist was not afraid.

"Yes, though I walk through the valley of the *shadow* of death." To the psalmist, death was just a *shadow*, not the real thing. He did not deny the reality that a human being goes through the experience called death, but death is never really real to us who are believers. It is a transition, the process we go through to enter eternal life.

Shadow? Guess what? That is a positive word because if you see a *shadow*, you can be sure there is a sun! Or a bright light! There is a light behind every *shadow*.

The ultimate reality is what lies beyond death. There is a transcending life and a world "out there." We live in a spiritual universe. It is easy to imagine this when you look up in the sky and you know how many satellites and messages are there. What's in the air all around us? The songs? And the music? All of the messages and music and power that are transmitting through air and space.

One of my dear friends, John Wimber, is in heaven today. John was a great secular musician with the Righteous Brothers and was very, very successful. Then he found faith and began thinking about God and Jesus Christ, and he became a believer. He started reading the Bible and was impressed with how Jesus performed miracles. People who were sick were healed. So John started his own little church to pray for the sick to be healed, and to pray for miracles. That ministry, known as the Vineyard Ministry, is around the world today.

When John became ill with cancer, he used all the medical help available, and his people around the globe prayed for the miracle of healing, which was such a trademark of his ministry. But God didn't answer their prayers with a yes. The cancer returned, and this time it would be terminal. John was able to go back into his pulpit with his cancer still very alive. On his first Sunday back he said, "I have been in the valley, and I can tell you the view from the valley is not too bad."

There's Life Beyond Hope

Some of you don't like this ending. You prayed. You believed. Your heart was torn to pieces. You tried to trust. But it all ended. Death. Divorce. "Life's not fair," you say with a touch of bitterness.

"True," I reply, adding, "life's not fair—but God is good."[2]

Give God more time. Life's too short for all scores to be settled.

There is life beyond hope. Justice demands it. We can't accept an evil man like Hitler using suicide and getting off so easily with death. And we can't believe that God who is just and merciful can allow sin and evil to get by without facing ultimate justice.

God will not allow death to be a loophole!

He doesn't close the books on a life that dies. He opens the book of justice and mercy. He reigns eternally and will appropriately reward the faithful and apply justice where it is appropriate.

Give God more time, and eternity will balance everything beautifully.

Prepare to embrace eternity!

I believe that human souls live eternally. I embrace that belief even though I know very little about heaven and hell. But evidence both inside and outside Scripture hints of heaven. The disciples reported an amazing experience when they witnessed two persons appearing to Christ—Moses and Elijah, who had died centuries before. I recalled that recently when I read an amazing report, which seemed to testify to life beyond death.

Doctor Lori Wiener has specialized in caring for children dying with AIDS. Let this medical scientist add her word to the faith that gives ultimate comfort.

Working with children who have AIDS and their parents often challenges one's basic faith—whether a child is going to die, or a parent is going to die before a child. The children, even the young children, talk about what they think dying and the afterlife are like. When one of them is actually taking his or her last breath, and I'm with him, I pray for a peaceful transition. My belief in God, and in the power of God, helps me to achieve peace in the midst of the whole dying process. However, my spiritual life did not lead me to do the work I am doing. It is my work that has given me a deeper spiritual side.

I think that the reason my work has deepened my faith in God is because the children I work with talk about their experiences so vividly and spiritually. There is one story that moved me tremendously. A little girl was sitting down at the table with her mom, eating soup, and all of a sudden she just looked up and stared into space. She moved her eyes like she was following something, then she picked up her hand and started waving. She said, "Bye-bye, Allen. Bye-bye." The girl's mother said to her, "Honey, what are you doing?" And the girl said, "I'm saying good-bye to Allen. He's with Jesus." So the mom said, "Allen is fine, honey. Allen is fine." Less than a half hour later, the phone rang to say that Allen had died.

So many children and parents report stories like this to me. A child might say, "Someone's come to visit me a few times." Then the child would see, in a photo album, a photograph of someone who had died and say, "That's the person who has been visiting." Or they say a deceased brother or sister has come back, and they did things together.

One child, who was fourteen at the time, actually gave me the name of a child who had died a year and a half earlier, and he told me that these two children had come to visit him the night before. He said they had just walked straight through the window, and he showed me the window. He said, "They just came straight through and they told me that I shouldn't give up at this point, that although people don't think I have any more time, I still do. It's not my time yet." This child was very sick at the time, and I remember asking him what the experience was like for him. I asked him if it was frightening. And it wasn't. He said it was very comforting. He wanted the dead children's parents to know that the children are well, what they looked like, and what they said they were doing.

I have asked the children, "Tell me how they talk to you." And they have said, "I hear everything they say, but they never move their lips." I always ask this question, and over the years I have yet to hear someone tell me that the person who has come back to visit him or her has ever moved his or her lips. I don't know what that means. For most of the people, it has been very comforting. Frequently, when a person is very close to death, and he or she tells me that people who have died are in the room; my experience has been that usually, within hours, this person is going to die too.

Through my experiences with these children, I have developed a very strong sense of God's presence, and a very strong belief that this is one life, and there's a transition to another existence from here. From the stories I consistently hear, it has all been very positive, and there's no sense of time. The children tell me that they are told from the kids who come back to visit that the transition is going to seem really fast, that it won't feel like days, weeks, or months have gone by, that there is no reason to worry."[3]

Elements in this remarkable account sound familiar to Christians who have accepted as reality the biblical account of Jesus rising from the dead, passing through walls, appearing and speaking to His disciples, all of which I honestly believe happened!

Yes, there is life beyond hope. Yes, there is a God. He will have the last word—and it will be beautiful. Yes, there was a Man of God named Jesus Christ who lived. That's a fact. He died. That's a fact. He was resurrected from the dead. That's a mystery. He is my Lord and Savior. That's my faith. He has promised to all humans: "The one who comes to Me I will by no means cast out" (John 6:37). Holding to that promise, I face death and eternity knowing that I'm going where Jesus already is!

That's eternal life. That's salvation.

The other day my daughter Gretchen came to get her daughter, our granddaughter, Julia, who was visiting us, and she said, "Julia, it's time to come home."

Julia replied, "Why, is it dinner time?"

"No."

"Why, are we going someplace?"

"No, Julia, it's just time to come home."

"Okay, Mommy, I'll come home."

So she reached her little hand up to the larger hand of her mother, smiled, and waved, "Good-bye, Grandpa."

Well, we will all come to the time when we will hear the words, *It's time to come home*.

"Why?"

Because it's time to come home.

"Are we going someplace?"

Yes. *We're going to heaven.*

That's how life ends for the believer! Jesus Christ comes, and we walk off together to our happy eternal home.

As we look toward this final journey, we can hold on to the truth in the Twenty-third Psalm. A wise father once shared this truth with his son, a young university student who said when he came home from his secular studies, "I've lost my faith, Dad."

"Son, you haven't lost your faith; you are simply but seriously disconnected from a personal faith with the Lord. Read the Twenty-third Psalm. You can have more faith in these words than in the words of your secular cynical professors and negative-thinking fellow students. Son, read the words with emphasis on the personal relationship. God lives in these words, and He will bless you."

With that, the father handed his son these words, which focus on the personal relationship where faith is born.

The Lord is
MY
shepherd;
I
shall not want.
He makes
ME
to lie down
in green pastures;
He leads
ME
beside the still
waters.
He restores
MY
soul; He leads
ME
in the paths of
righteousness for
His name's sake.
Yea, though
I

walk through the valley
of the shadow of death,
I
will fear no evil;
For You are with
ME;
Your rod and Your staff,
they comfort
ME.
You prepare a table before
ME
in the presence of
MY
enemies; You anoint
MY
head with oil;
MY
cup runs over.
Surely goodness and mercy
shall follow
ME
all the days of
MY
life.
And . . .
I
will dwell in

the house of the LORD
forever.

Get personal and get connected with Jesus Christ. You will have life beyond hope! And you will turn your hurts into halos!

A Closing Prayer for You

MARY HAYS-BRIDGES was accepted into the Air Force Academy, and her mentor, the moon walker Jim Irwin, thought she would be the first woman astronaut. In her second year at the academy, however, Mary suffered a fall that not only forced her out of school but also led to fifty-six surgeries over the next twenty years.

I became Mary's pastor when her dad died; she was only thirteen. For all of those years after her accident—through the pain and surgeries—I was with her. I wrote a prayer for her, recorded it, and she lived with it through two decades of pain. Frankly, I had forgotten the prayer; after all, it was twenty years old! As I finished this book, Mary gave it to me to share how prayer kept her optimism alive.

Today Mary is the first person in medical history to have her spine rebuilt with titanium braces. She plans to run in the Pike's Peak Marathon. She is totally, completely pain-free! Now Mary shares "her" prayer with you.

You never promised, Lord, that I would be forever sheltered from stormy times in my life.

You have promised that the sun will outlast the storms.

You issue the grand command from outer space, and the renegade storm clouds break up, scatter, and flee like hoodlums hurriedly racing from the streets back to their hidden lairs in some forbidden alley.

The bright stars come out to laugh again like children returning once more to safe streets for happy play. The sky clears. The huge yellow moon sails once more, calm and serene, through the silent sky.

Even as You restore peace after the storm, so You will restore a renewed calm to my troubled mind through Your peace-instilling presence that is surrounding me now.

Your quiet, calming spirit is flowing within me. Thank You, Lord.

Thank You, God, for dangers that teach me to be brave . . .
for suffering, from which I learn patience . . .
for pain, which teaches me tenderness . . .
for false friends, whose lack of trust causes me to prize my true friends . . .
for illness, which teaches me to treasure my health, a gift I too often take for granted.

Thank You for leading me through trying times, without which I would be like a plant in an overprotected hothouse, too tender to ever live in the open wind.

Help me to remember in my trying times that there is
no progress without pain,
no conversion without crisis,
no birth without painful travail,
no Easter without Good Friday.

Trying times are times to try more faith. I'm trying. I'm believing. You are helping me.

Thank You, Lord.
Amen

Notes

CHAPTER 1

1. This quotation is from "Because He Lives," words by Gloria Gaither. © Copyright 1971 by William J. Gaither.
2. Helen Keller as quoted by J. Wallace Hamilton, *What About Tomorrow?* (Grand Rapids, MI: Fleming H. Revell Co., 1972).

CHAPTER 5

1. The Pee Wee Kirkland story is based on an article that appeared in *Parade* magazine, July 13, 1997, 22–23.

CHAPTER 8

1. "Jesus Loves Me," words by Anna B. Warner (1820–1915).

CHAPTER 10

1. Joanna Laufer and Kenneth S. Lewis, *Inspired: The Breath of God* (New York: Doubleday, 1998), 5.
2. Robert H. Schuller, *Life's Not Fair, but God Is Good* (Nashville:Thomas Nelson Publishers, 1991).
3. Ibid., 20–21.

About the Author

Dr. Robert Schuller is a pastor, speaker, motivator, and author whose positive messages are a source of strength and hope for millions of people around the world. Every Sunday Dr. Schuller is seen and heard by an estimated thirty million persons on the *Hour of Power,* the most widely televised one-hour church service in the world.

In 1955, Dr. Schuller was called by the Reformed Church in America to begin a new church in Garden Grove, California. With his wife, Arvella, as the organist and $500 in assets, he rented the Orange Drive-in Theater and conducted Sunday services from the tar-papered roof of the snack bar. That first Sunday, 100 persons—all sitting in their cars—attended. Dr. Schuller, who believes this outdoor ministry experience helped inspire him to later build the first-ever, all-glass Crystal Cathedral, often says, “It was there I fell in love with the sky!”

Dr. Schuller is senior pastor of the Crystal Cathedral, a congregation with over 10,000 members. He is also the author of thirty-two books, including five best-sellers.